The Leadership Path

A Guide for Leading Yourself, Your
Team, and Your Organisation

Blake Repine

Published in Australia in 2023 by Blake Repine

Website: https://www.blakerepine.com.au

© Blake Repine 2023

The moral right of the author has been asserted.

All rights reserved.

Except as permitted under the *Australian Copyright Act 1968* (for example, a fair dealing for the purposes of study, research, criticism or review), no part of this publication may be reproduced, stored in a retrieval system, communicated or transmitted in any form or by any means without prior written permission.

All enquiries should be directed to the author.

ISBN 9780648841227 (paperback)
ISBN 9780648841234 (ebook)

 A catalogue record for this book is available from the National Library of Australia

Disclaimer

The author has made every effort to ensure the accuracy of the information within this book was correct at the time of publication. The author does not assume and hereby disclaims any liability to any party for any loss, damage or disruption caused by errors or omissions, whether such errors or omissions result from accident, negligence, or any other cause.

This book is dedicated to my son, James.
You have taught me so much about passion and creativity. I am thankful that I get to be a part of your life's journey and watch you grow; it is my greatest adventure. I am proud to be your father and I hope that you achieve all your goals, realise all your dreams, and live a fulfilling life. You are now, and will always be, my greatest success.
I love you, son.

Acknowledgements

Once again, I would like to thank my editor, Judy Gregory, for helping me find my voice and for helping me to continue to grow as an author. I would also like to thank Rachel Freeman for being my proofreader, sounding board and supporter throughout the development of this book.

Contents

Introduction   1

SECTION ONE – Leading Self   7
  What is Leadership?   8
  Be Aware of Leadership Myths   11
  Be a Student for Life   16
  Cultivate a Growth Mindset   21
  Plan Your Next Step   35
  Everything in Life is a Trade-Off   38
  Only You Can Define Your Success   41
  Have Your Own Personal Value Proposition   46
  Be the Hero of Your Own Story   51
  There's No Such Thing as a Stress-Free Life   54
  Look After Yourself   58
  What Is Resilience?   65
  Relationships Are Powerful   69
  Quit Trying to Get People to Like You   73
  Quit Trying to Be Perfect   78
  Address Imposter Syndrome   82

    Watch Out for Unconscious Bias   86
    Cultivate Moral Courage   92
    Use Your Authority Responsibly   96
    Never Say: 'That's Not My Job'   100

SECTION TWO – Leading Teams and Organisations   105
    4 Steps to Building Your Tribe   108
    Are You Leading or Managing?   111
    Balance Compliance Versus Commitment   117
    Communicate with Your Team   122
    Focus on Your People   128
    Let Others Hold You Accountable   133
    Managing Up – and Why You Should Do It   136
    Your Industry Isn't Special   144
    6 Principles for KPIs   148
    The Value of Money   153
    Most Decisions Are Made with Emotion   155
    TED Talks and Other Difficult Conversations   157
    Get Comfortable with Silence   163
    What Is Strategic Thinking?   165
    Organisational Culture Is Your Responsibility   168

Conclusion   174

Suggested Reading   177

About the Author   179

Introduction

In mid-2022, I was asked to give a keynote speech at a local high school for their graduation. It was a different type of speech to the ones I'd done in the past.

I don't consider myself to be an expert public speaker. In fact, as you'll see in the chapter titled 'TED Talks and Other Difficult Conversations', it's not something I've previously enjoyed. But over time I've learned about how good presentations work and practised a lot, and I've become quite comfortable with delivering things like keynote presentations at corporate retreats and conferences.

For this high school graduation, I spent some time thinking about what I could say that would be interesting and relevant for young people who were leaving school. I went hunting for some nugget of inspiration or advice that might be relevant to them.

Leadership has long been a topic that's interested me – and it's the topic I've written about most extensively. But I wasn't initially sure how I could make my thoughts about leadership relevant to a group of teenagers who were about to embark on their adult life.

Eventually, I started to think about the relevance of leadership to my everyday life, and that got me thinking about whether any of my life lessons had shaped my perspectives on leadership. I see leadership as something that applies in every aspect of life. It's not restricted to the workplace – it spills over into my family life, my personal relationships, and my sense of self.

I believe there's a direct correlation between how people manage their personal lives and how they manage their work lives. People who are good managers of their personal lives will often be good managers in the workplace.

I also believe that leadership is something we're constantly learning. It's like a permanent apprenticeship, with increasing mastery but with no end point. We learn both from structured learning like school and university, and from the various situations we find ourselves in. How we react to the situations we encounter shapes both our personal worldviews and our leadership focus.

With that in mind, I attempted to take my years of life experience and condense them down into a presentation for the high school graduation. And it was while I was talking to the students that I had a little lightbulb moment: maybe these ideas were worth sharing more widely! That's how this book came into being.

In this book, I've assembled the things that matter to me when I think about leadership. It's broken down into two sections, each with a distinct focus:

Leading self

Leading teams and organisations.

My hope is that these ideas will help you – no matter where you are on your leadership journey.

This book is about developing a leadership mindset, which is relevant for all types of leadership. It doesn't matter whether your goal is to lead an organisation, a community group, or your personal relationships. This book provides an approach to leadership that will help you to think about what's important for you and what you still need to learn.

My hope is that my experiences and thoughts about leadership will help you to reflect on and cultivate your own leadership skills and practice. I don't set out to develop a comprehensive list of everything that's important for a leader. Instead, I want to share some of my thoughts and experiences to help you reflect on your own. I hope these ideas will help to make your leadership journey a little easier than it otherwise would be. I've included the things I wish I'd known earlier.

Success doesn't come easy. Often, we learn more from failures than we do from successes. But even knowing that, failures still hurt, and they can still knock your confidence. More often than not, life is a complex combination of little successes and little failures or challenges. These are all learning opportunities, helping you to develop your skills and contributing to your depth of experience.

This book doesn't describe a path for guaranteed success or great riches. I don't pretend to have all the answers. All I have is my own thoughts, reflections, and experiences – based on many years of working in both the military and corporate life and based on my studies.

I hope you find something in this book that speaks to you and helps you along your path of developing as a leader. If you finish this book and feel you've developed your leadership skills or adapted your thinking – even in the smallest way – then I'll have accomplished my goal.

SECTION ONE

Leading Self

For us to be able to lead others, we must first be able to lead ourselves. Leading the self is the foundation of all leadership. This doesn't mean that leaders must live perfect lives – quite the opposite!

Throughout our lives, we are all faced with situations and decisions that challenge us. We won't always make the right decisions, but we will always have to live with the consequences of these decisions – whether good or bad. Regardless of the outcome, we learn. And through learning, we continuously shore up the foundation of our leadership abilities and make them stronger.

If leading the self is the foundation of all leadership, then the ability to learn and reflect is the mechanism that strengthens the foundation. That is why this section of the book is the largest by far.

The principles listed in this section are by no means a complete list of the attributes that matter when it comes to self leadership. Instead, they're a compilation of the more prominent things that seem particularly important to me. I'm sure that as I continue my leadership journey, I'll continue to grow and develop my understanding of these attributes. And I hope you're able to do the same.

What Is Leadership?

Leadership is one of those things that we recognise but find difficult to clearly define. There is no universally agreed definition of leadership – though common themes emerge from the various definitions I've read. In this section, I discuss some of those common themes and explain why I think they're important.

- Leadership is earned: You're only a leader if you've got people who follow you and believe in you. This means that leadership is something that's granted by the team, not given through a job title or the corner office. If you have a leadership title, but there's no one following you, you're not actually a leader.
- Leaders inspire others: They motivate people to do things.
- Leaders lead by example: They inspire people through their actions. What they do is strongly connected with what they say.
- Leaders provide vision.
- Leaders rally people around a shared purpose.
- Leaders provide guidance and direction.
- Leaders help people to remove roadblocks.

- Leaders help their team to develop themselves.
- Leaders are values led: Great leaders understand that people need to see strong values such as trust, credibility, and integrity.
- Leaders demonstrate empathy.
- Leaders are resilient: They keep working during difficult times and bounce back quickly after a failure.
- Leaders demonstrate passion: Zig Ziglar once said that passion is what people have when they realise their potential.[1]
- Leaders listen more than they talk: They listen to multiple aspects of conversations, not just the most obvious content.
- Leaders are flexible and understanding: They understand that sometimes the team will need to deviate from its path, even if the end objective hasn't changed. Good leaders have enough flexibility to respond to emerging issues, but not so much flexibility that they lose sight of the objective.
- Leaders are fair and impartial: They don't show favourites within the team; they understand the difference between personal and professional relationships.
- Leaders are consistent: A good leader is the same person every day and their team can be confident about how the leader will approach an issue or react to a problem. They're not moody or unpredictable. Even when things are difficult, good leaders will be consistent in their decision-making and general conduct.

---

1. Zig Ziglar (1926–2012) was an American author and motivational speaker, famous for books such as *See You at the Top* and *Zig Ziglar's Secrets of Closing the Sale*.

- Leaders give praise and accept responsibility: Great leaders are happy to give praise to members of the team. They're selfless enough to recognise that success isn't just about them as an individual. But when things go wrong, great leaders accept responsibility. They recognise that no team is perfect, and they accept that they're the person who is ultimately responsible.
- Leaders have coaching qualities: Great leaders recognise strengths in other people and work to develop those strengths. Great leaders don't feel challenged by having smart and capable people on their team. They actively work to develop the next generation of leaders. They're not frightened of becoming redundant.
- Leaders are human: They make mistakes, just like the rest of us. Great leaders understand this and accept themselves as flawed but committed. The best leaders recognise their mistakes, learn from them, and move on.
- Leaders work for their team ahead of the organisation: A great leader recognises that their main responsibility is to the people who are on their team. A true leader doesn't work for an organisation – they work for the people employed by that organisation. They're accountable to everyone and feel responsible to everyone. In job interviews for CEO positions, I often ask candidates how many people they worked for in their last organisation. The most promising candidates say they worked for everyone in the organisation. The least promising candidates identify the board.

Be Aware of Leadership Myths

There are several myths surrounding leadership – that is, unfounded beliefs people have about certain things that will or won't happen when they become a leader or accept a leadership role in an organisation. I'd like to expose these beliefs for what they are: unfounded myths that might hamper your leadership potential.

MYTH: Leadership is based on your job title or position in the organisation

It's easy to think that leadership is a job title or position – that you apply for a leadership position, are successfully appointed to it, and simply become a leader when you weren't one before. Leadership is not like that. True leadership isn't a job title or a particular position within an organisation. Instead, leadership is based on how you interact with people – how you behave and how you treat others. Leadership is a quality that develops over time. It's something that others recognise in you. And while leaders typically hold senior positions in an organisation, that's not necessarily the case.

Sometimes there's a disconnect between the leadership skills required by a role and the leadership skills demonstrated by the individual in that role. Senior roles can be filled by people with no idea about leadership. And sometimes, true leaders are found working in junior roles.

MYTH: You can't lead from a junior position

It's easy to assume that people in junior positions are always followers. Perhaps they don't have the skill or ambition to become leaders and are happy to stay in a junior role. Or perhaps they're inexperienced, and their leadership potential is still developing – leadership is in their future. But this belief is based on a myth: it's a myth that it's impossible to lead from a junior position. Anyone, in any position, can demonstrate leadership.

Of course, in some organisations, people in junior positions who have leadership potential may be too scared to display their leadership skills. They may believe they won't be trusted or listened to. They may believe they don't have a right to speak out. But leadership skills and attributes can be demonstrated by anyone, and having people in junior positions who display leadership skills can be a great asset to an organisation. A useful book about this topic is *The 360 Degree Leader*, by John Maxwell.[2] Maxwell explores the idea of leading from any position within an organisation. Leadership isn't just about leading down through the hierarchy. There's also a valid place for leading up and for leading to the side.

---

2. *The 360 Degree Leader* by John C Maxwell, 2016, HarperCollins.

MYTH: When you're in a senior position, everyone will do what you say

If you're working in a senior or leadership position in an organisation, you may reasonably expect that everyone will do what you ask them to do. And of course, it's mostly true. If a senior manager asks for something to be done, it typically gets done.

But it's important to keep in mind that people don't have to do what you say. People choose what they listen to, and they choose what requests to enact. Even for the most senior leaders, control is an illusion.

Staff may be 'obedient' based on the potential consequences they'll face if they don't do what you ask. This means that your position and your ability to impose consequences become the reasons why people respond to your request. That's not a particularly positive way to get things done, and it tends to lead to just a minimal response by most people. Instead, it's best to achieve outcomes through positive motivation. If your staff share your vision for the business and if they recognise that your leadership is taking the business in the right direction, they're more likely to be motivated to do what you ask. They'll be motivated by your vision and your style, not by the command of your position.

Try to avoid using the authority of your position to get things done. Sometimes using authority might be unavoidable – such as in a crisis for example, or when there's a disagreement within the organisation. But most of the time, look for other ways to achieve outcomes. Find ways to interest and excite people about the work ahead.

MYTH: Once you're in a leadership position, you can do what you want

Leaders are not free to behave in whatever way they want. They are not exempt from the rules of good practice that apply to everyone else. Good leaders understand this, and lead by example.

People in senior roles are given concessions about certain things. They may have a bigger office, support staff, or a travel allowance. They'll almost certainly receive more pay. These things are designed to support them in the job they need to do. But the legal and compliance requirements of the workplace apply to everyone. In some cases, they're even more relevant to people in leadership positions.

People in leadership positions should provide strong examples of how they expect people to behave. If the leader is seen to be doing the wrong thing, why should anyone else in the organisation behave any differently? Staff members watch how leaders make decisions – particularly ethical and moral decisions that can be challenging – and they will mirror the behaviour they see. It doesn't make sense for a leader to behave one way but expect something different from staff.

MYTH: Once you're in a senior leadership role, your work gets easier

I'm not sure where this myth comes from, but quite a few people seem to think that life is easier in the corner office. There's a perception that senior leaders get more time to relax. It's simply not true.

Of course, the nature of work changes as you move up through an organisation. Most senior positions rely less on technical skills and more on interpersonal skills. And as the nature of work shifts towards a greater focus on interpersonal skills, the work typically increases in both volume and intensity. Senior leaders are busy people, who need to be ready to respond to requests from all levels of the organisation.

Don't see leadership as a fast track to an easier life. It isn't.

MYTH: You're only a leader at work

In some senior leadership roles, leadership responsibility can spread out of the workplace. Some leaders find that the way they conduct themselves in the wider community, and even in their private lives, can be of great interest to others. The more public facing your organisation is, the more relevant this will be. Also, the larger the organisation is, the more public scrutiny you may find yourself subject to.

I'm sure you can quickly think of several headlines where a c-suite executive was caught up in a scandal in their private lives that caused them to step down. I remember someone telling me that once you're in a high-level position, you must be beyond reproach. This isn't to say that you have to live a perfect life, but you do have to live within ethical standards.

Be a Student for Life

If there's one constant in life, it's change. And to keep up, you need to adopt the mindset of a keen, interested, engaged student. You need to be a student *of* life, *for* life.

I've been in the workforce for around 30 years, and during that time I've seen incredible technological advances. Every day, I now use technology that I couldn't even imagine 30 years ago. The pace of technological change doesn't show any sign of slowing down. If anything, it's getting faster each year. If you're not an engaged student, you'll get left behind.

Accept the learning curve

We all experience a learning curve every time we're faced with a new technology or a new idea about how to work. We constantly need to adapt to new ways of working. If you adopt a student mindset, you'll be ready to embrace the learning curve and enjoy the challenge of learning something new.

For most people, the learning curve is most obvious when you start a new job – that's when you meet new people, learn new ways of working, and adapt to new systems. There might be a lot to learn, and you might need time to adapt. It's easier if you approach it as a student, keen to learn something new.

It's the same in your wider life too. The first time you buy a house or a car, or the first time you play a new sport, you need to learn new skills and adapt to challenges. At first, doing something new can be difficult. But each time you do the new thing, it becomes a little bit easier. You gradually move up the learning curve.

See new experiences as opportunities

A keen, engaged student recognises every experience as an opportunity for learning. If you practise a student's mindset, you'll be able to take advantage of challenges, learn new things, and apply those learnings in the future.

It's easy enough to learn when you experience success – most people are good at reflecting on what they did well and thinking about how they can learn to repeat their successes. But it's also important to learn from failures and struggles. Everyone experiences difficulties and everyone needs to navigate through problems, and these can be great opportunities for learning.

When you experience challenges, try to take some time to reflect. Think about what caused the struggle and how you can grow from the experience. Then the next time you face a similar struggle, you'll be one step ahead.

Embrace opportunities to learn

We live in an age when the opportunity to learn is at our fingertips every day. For most topics, great lessons are freely available via YouTube. I love the way I can go to YouTube and find someone with experience – someone who has faced a particular challenge before and has taken the time to make a video explaining the best way forward. It seems that any time I want to learn a new skill – whether it's how to build a website, learn coding, get better at photography, or think about how to deal with conflict – there's a niche video about the topic already available on YouTube.

YouTube is a great asset, but obviously it can't teach you immediate mastery of a new skill. When you start doing something new, you're not likely to be perfect. That's ok. The more you practise, the better you'll get. In many cases, you don't need to be perfect to get great results.

There's a popular idea that you need to practise 10,000 repetitions or do something for 10,000 hours to get anywhere near perfection.[3] I've heard that Michael Jordon used to take 100 free throw shots every session, just to improve his skill.

I like the idea that amateurs practise until they get something right, and professionals practise until they can't get it wrong. It's not that the professional is perfect – they all recognise they could be better – but they practise so much that the skills and movements are second nature. They can perform without thinking because the skill has become an integral part of themselves.

If you have a student mindset, you'll recognise that practice (or study) is essential. You'll also recognise that practice is something that doesn't end. Once you've almost perfected something, you can only remain at peak performance if you continue to practise. Without it, you'll lose the skill.

Believe in yourself

It's tempting to think that learning a new skill is too difficult and that you'll never be able to master whatever it is that you're trying to achieve. But if that's your attitude, you've failed before you've even begun.

---

3. The idea that it takes 10,000 hours of practice to develop mastery was popularised by Malcolm Gladwell in his 2008 book *Outliers: The Story of Success* (Penguin).

A tendency to acceptance failure without even trying is something I see a lot in workplaces. I'll ask people if they've ever used a system or a particular skill, and they'll automatically dismiss it by saying they don't know how to do that and couldn't possibly learn.

If you dismiss something without trying, then you're right – you won't ever learn. But if you have the mindset of a student, and if you approach new tasks with an open mind, there's every chance that you'll learn something new. With practice and repetition, you'll become a master.

The best way to learn new skills is to be open to possibility. Believe in yourself. Believe in your ability to learn new things. Accept that it may be difficult at first, and be willing to practise, and practise, then practise some more.

Stretch yourself

If you have a student mindset, you'll be willing to stretch yourself – and that will help you to succeed in things you didn't think were possible.

Workplaces often have a pile of tasks that have been put in the 'too hard basket'. No one is sure what to do, so they remain unsolved. But all it takes is for one person to put up their hand and offer to give it a go.

I've done that a few times in different jobs. There will be some workplace challenge that everyone has been avoiding, and I'll be the one who offers to find a solution. There's nothing special about me – I'm just a typical worker of average intelligence. But what I do have is the mindset of a student, combined with a strong work ethic, an ability to learn, and persistence to keep trying when things seem too hard. I just keep asking questions and calling on experts until I figure out the solution. I take the project one step at a time, and I don't give up until the problem is solved. The result is that I've ended up with a reputation as the guy who can solve challenging tasks.

Having the mindset of a student – *of* life and *for* life – is an important thinking strategy for any leader. Try to combine it with a willingness to try new ideas and an acceptance that things will change. If you approach everything with this mindset, you will be able to accomplish nearly anything.

Cultivate a Growth Mindset

I'm often struck by the way children approach the world. Most children naturally have what business theorists would call a 'growth mindset'. Children want to learn about everything. Their appetite for new knowledge sometimes seems insatiable.

I guess there are two reasons why children are ready to learn. Firstly, they don't know a lot, so learning things is interesting and new. Most children have a burning desire to understand how the world works and understand their position in it. Secondly, they don't have a lot of experience, so they're frequently experiencing new things. New things are exciting, and children get to experience that excitement regularly. When children ask 'why', 'why', 'why' about anything and everything, they're not trying to annoy the adult around them. Instead, they're revelling in the joy of learning new things.

But the joy of learning new things is something that many adults seem to forget. Most adults stop asking 'why' and stop trying to find new experiences. Many adults learn a trade or become experienced in a particular field, then just continue to do similar things every day until they reach retirement. For many, life throws up few experiences that could be truly described as new. Of course, there's a certain level of professional development and experience gathering going on for most adults, but it's not the type of transformative, growth-mindset learning that children engage in. What happens for many adults is that their learning curve flatlines. And for many people, that's a recipe for dissatisfaction.

Your brain doesn't get full

Some adults claim that they can't continue to learn new things because their brains get full and there's no space left to take on new ideas. I don't buy into that view. I think it's impossible to have a full brain, just like I think it's impossible to exhaust the variety of things out there to be learned.

So perhaps a reasonable question for adults is – what exactly is a growth mindset, and how can we cultivate it throughout life? How can we approach life in a way that pushes us to stretch our boundaries and try new things?

Being inspired by Dweck

I've been inspired by the work of Carol Dweck and her book *Mindset: The New Psychology of Success*.[4] In the book, Dweck writes about how, in some settings, effort is seen as a bad thing – it's like failure because it suggests that you're not smart or talented. If you were smart or talented, you wouldn't need to make so much effort.

But Dweck notes that, in other settings, effort is what leads to you being recognised as smart and talented. And that's the world I belong to. I believe that putting in effort is what leads to results. You don't need to be smarter than

---

4. *Mindset: The New Psychology of Success. How We Can Learn to Fulfill Our Potential* by Carol S Dweck, 2006, Random House.

everyone else or more talented than everyone else. You just need to be smart enough and talented enough to get by. Most of all, you need to be willing to put in above-average effort. That's what makes the difference.

Sometimes I wonder whether smart people are prone to wasting their intelligence. Recently, I was reading about the eight different types of intelligence, each linked to a different way of processing information. The eight types are called: logical-mathematical intelligence, linguistic intelligence, spatial intelligence, musical intelligence, bodily-kinesthetic intelligence, intrapersonal intelligence, interpersonal intelligence, and naturalistic intelligence.[5] The thing that struck me is that everyone scores differently on each type of intelligence, and scoring high in one type doesn't necessarily influence your score in another. People are more likely to become exceptionally good in things that build on their natural type of intelligence.

This all suggests that it doesn't make sense to simply rate intelligence in terms of your ability to do mathematics or read literature. You could have intelligence for music and art. Or you could have intelligence for designing things, building things, creating things, or working with your hands. Some people have intelligence for details. Other people have intelligence for strategy.

But whatever type of intelligence you have, you have to wonder whether it's wasted if it's not accompanied by effort.

---

5. The eight types of intelligence were first discussed by Harvard University psychologist Howard Gardner, in his 1983 book *Frames of Mind* (Basic Books). I read about them in an article by Kumar Mehta, titled 'A Harvard Psychologist Says Humans Have 8 Types of Intelligence. Which Ones Do You Score the Highest in?', 10 March 2021, *CNBC MakeIt* (https://www.cnbc.com/2021/03/10/harvard-psychologist-types-of-intelligence-where-do-you-score-highest-in.html).

It's effort that creates a growth mindset, not intelligence – whatever type of intelligence you have.

People who have a growth mindset tend to be persistent and committed. They also tend to keep learning when other people might give up. Eventually, they'll master whatever subject they're working on and become an expert in their field. The old rule of thumb is probably true: achieving anything is 90 per cent effort and 10 per cent either intelligence or luck. It's effort that makes the difference.

In a short article, Saga Briggs sums up Dweck's work by suggesting ways to develop a growth mindset.[6] You don't have to apply them all – applying just some of them will probably make a great difference. I'm summarising them here so you can choose the ones that make most sense for you.

1. Acknowledge and embrace imperfections: If you hide from your weaknesses, you'll never overcome them; in contrast, if you recognise your weaknesses you'll become comfortable with them and be able to work to your strengths.

2. View challenge as opportunities: Relish in and embrace challenges that provide opportunities for self-improvement; accept challenges as opportunities to build confidence and get better at things.

3. Try different learning tactics: You may assume that you learn best in a certain way, but sometimes you have to try a new learning strategy to master something new; change things up a bit and give things a go. Remember that different people learn in different ways.

---

6. '25 Ways to Develop a Growth Mindset' by Saga Briggs, 10 February 2015, *InformEd* (http://www.opencolleges.edu.au/informed/features/develop-a-growth-mindset/).

4. Follow research on brain plasticity: Remember that your brain is a muscle and it needs to work out just like every other muscle in your body. Make it work! The more you exercise it, the fitter it will get. You don't need to do specific brain-training exercises. Just have fun and learn new things!

5. Replace 'failing' with 'learning': When you don't quite reach a goal, remember that you haven't failed, you've learned. When you don't quite achieve something, focus on what you learned from the experience rather than what you didn't get. Each time you 'learn', you'll find it easier to achieve next time.

6. Stop seeking approval: This is one that I particularly like because it reminds me to prioritise my own growth, not the approval I can get from others. It reminds me that I don't need to follow social norms or make other people think I'm doing the right thing. What matters is that I'm feeling comfortable about the achievements I make. It reminds me that seeking approval from others is temporary and false.

7. Value the process over the end result: People with a growth mindset simply love to learn. It often doesn't matter what they're learning or why, they simply enjoy learning new things.

8. Cultivate a sense of purpose: For me, this is about keeping the big picture in mind and feeling that my life has a sense of direction. It means I have a purpose in life and a complete mindset about life in general. It's the reason for getting out of bed on a Monday morning.

9. Celebrate growth in others: I recognise that this isn't always easy, but there's a lot of satisfaction in helping other people to grow and helping them celebrate their achievements. I get to experience this in the gym, when I help people learn how to lift heavy weights. But I've also achieved it at work. It's hugely satisfying to help people achieve their career aspirations – they don't owe you anything, but you can celebrate alongside them when they achieve.

10. Emphasise growth over speed: This is about recognising that learning and growth take time. Learning new things can be difficult, and any new skill usually requires a huge amount of practice. For example, in the sport of Olympic lifting, it takes at least three to five years to become good at weightlifting – that's the investment required before most people can become competitive. With weightlifting the trade-off is clear: if you try to build too fast, you'll simply injure yourself; you must grow at a pace that's slow and steady. Another good analogy is weight loss – you can't lose 25 kilograms in a few weeks; the best, safest, and most reliable approach is to lose the weight slowly. Any learning should be the same. You must be patient. You must build strong habits and make the new activity sustainable. Growth isn't fast. Big achievements aren't fast. You need to forget about instant gratification. You can't become a doctor overnight. You can't become a leader overnight either.

11. Reward actions, not traits: We already know that big achievements take time and practice. The amount of practice you need and the pace at which you gain mastery will vary for everyone because

everyone grows at a different pace. The logical extension of that idea is that it makes sense to reward your action, not your outputs. If you reward your effort and the time you invest in whatever it is you're trying to achieve, you'll be rewarding yourself for something that's truly meaningful. It's the effort you're making that earns you the reward, not the things you achieve. Some people need to set external rewards to keep themselves motivated – perhaps a special thing they'll do when they reach a certain milestone. But many people discover that the action itself is sufficient reward. If you focus on celebrating your actions ahead of your output, you may find that the action itself become intrinsically self-motivating.

12. Redefine genius: I've already referred to the idea that people have different types of intelligence. Genius is the same – it comes in different types and manifests in different ways. Being recognised as a genius means that you've achieved the top level of intelligence or performance in a particular area – beyond what is achieved by most people. To achieve a genius level takes work. Nobody is born with all the knowledge or ability to achieve anything at a very high level. At some point, everyone had to start learning at the beginning. It's important to recognise that genius is developed over time and with experience. It's based on understanding and application, and is not necessarily linked to intellect. Yes, some people learn more quickly than others – perhaps because they're playing to their strengths. Just remember that genius is more closely linked to hard work than it is to talent.

13. Portray criticism as positive: It's easy to be critical of others, and it's easy to believe that any criticism you receive is negative. It's so easy to slip into a negative mindset and assume that any criticism means you must be doing something wrong. But things might look different if you simply assume that criticism is a well-meant form of feedback, designed to help you improve at whatever it is you're trying to achieve. Accepting criticism as positive can be hard work, but it's well worth it. When you see criticism through a positive lens, you'll be much more able to learn from it. I know how difficult this can be. Like many people, I've experienced criticism that I've taken to be highly negative. Sometimes the criticism is clearly coming from a bad place or being delivered with ill intent – perhaps because the person giving it is jealous or resentful. In those circumstances, I try to understand why the person felt they needed to criticise, and I examine my actions for the grain of truth the criticism is likely to contain. But most criticism is well meant, and I work hard to see it for what it is – nothing more than an opportunity to improve.

14. Dissociate improvement from failure: It's important to recognise that having room for improvement doesn't mean you're a failure. Most of us have room to improve in pretty much everything. And if we work hard, we'll continue to improve. The polar opposite of failure isn't simply success. It's every step in the journey of improvement. When you cultivate a growth mindset, you realise there's always room for improvement. And from that mindset, it doesn't make sense to feel that gradual improvement is linked to failure.

15. Provide regular opportunities for reflection: It's important to take time out to reflect on your progress and assess whether anything needs to change. I like to do this any time I've had a difficult conversation or completed a task where the outcome wasn't quite what I expected. But I also like to build in reflection time when things are going well. I try to take a few minutes at the end of each day to reflect on what I've done that day and ask myself questions about what I've achieved, whether I could have done anything differently, and whether there are any opportunities for change that I need to think about. Sometimes I make a few notes that I hope will guide me next time I encounter a similar situation.

16. Place effort before talent: Work ethic and effort trump talent every day. It applies to athletes and it applies to leaders. When I'm training a weightlifter, I prefer to take on someone who shows up for training every day and who is ready to put in the hours. I always prefer the hard worker over the naturally talented athlete who is lazy and doesn't understand how to work. And the reason is simple. In the long run, effort trumps talent. Focus on becoming someone who has the right mindset and is willing to put in the hours. Give up worrying about whether you were born with talent. It's ok to have average talent and average intelligence; just accompany those traits with commitment and hard work.

17. Cultivate grit: People with grit have the ability to take the knocks that life throws in their path. They get knocked down, and they get back up and try again. When you cultivate grit, you grow in confidence and in the ability to achieve. It helps

you realise just how tough you really are. If you're interested in this topic, you might like to read the book *Grit* by Angela Duckworth.[7] One way to cultivate grit is to work on slow, gradual improvements and compete against yourself. I've done this with weightlifting: I compete against myself by lifting slightly heavier weights and keeping track of my progress. Sometimes I go backwards – with a little injury or some interruption to my training – but my past experiences in training have given me the confidence to get right back at it.

18. Abandon the image: An image is an end goal – some sort of idealised impression of what you might be like in the future, or what your future life might be like. This image is a fiction. And the distance between where you are today and how you'll achieve that image is likely to be poorly defined. Instead of focusing on that fictional end goal, focus on today. What do you need to do right now? What's the next feasible step in the journey you're trying to take? Focus on concrete steps that take you in the right direction, and abandon the idea that the end goal will be some type of nirvana. It's highly likely that you'll discover the end goal doesn't even exist as a fixed idea – it simply keeps moving ahead as you approach it.

19. Use the word 'yet': If you're struggling with something or if you're conscious that there's something you'd like to achieve in the future, accept that your achievement hasn't happened yet. It's not that you won't do it or that you can't do it. It's definitely not

---

7. *Grit: The Power of Passion and Perseverance* by Angela Duckworth, 2017, Vermilion.

that you're no good at it. The best perspective is simply to accept that you haven't achieved it *yet* – you're working towards it, and you still have some way to go. As long as you keep working towards that goal, you'll continue to move yourself closer. And that's what helps you to keep your focus.

20. Learn from other people's mistakes: It's helpful to find out about the setbacks and mistakes experienced by other people – in addition to learning about their successes, of course. Setbacks and mistakes can provide valuable lessons, and learning from other people may help you to avoid the same problems yourself. Don't be afraid to contact people and ask them questions about their various successes, mistakes, and setbacks. You could even ask people in your network whether there are three setbacks they've overcome that they'd be willing to share with you.

21. Make a new goal every time you achieve a current goal: It's helpful to always be working towards something, and one of the best ways to do this is to set a new goal each time you achieve an existing goal – preferably something that builds on what you've just achieved. While it's helpful to make your goals time-bound (that is, you plan to achieve this goal within a specific timeframe), there's no need to restrict yourself to 12-monthly goals. If you set 12-monthly goals and achieve them all in eight months, does that simply mean you take a four-month holiday? It makes more sense to set a new goal straight away. If you keep setting new goals, you'll keep moving yourself forward. This applies to

your business and your life at work just as much as it applies to any other type of goal.

22. Take risks in the company of others: Some people avoid taking risks in the company of others because they don't want to be judged. They get so caught up with worrying about how other people will react to them, that they fail to take a risk that offers a great opportunity. If possible, put aside your worries about being judged, and be willing to take risks that others will see. This is particularly important if you're terrified of public speaking. Take the risk and get out there – you'll probably find that it's better than you expect.

I was recently at a conference with around 800 delegates, linked to an organisation that I'd only just joined. I had been nominated for a vice-president's role, and the election was to take place at the conference. But as a newbie, no one in the organisation knew who I was. All the nominees were asked to give a three-minute speech to the 800 delegates. I started by commenting that none of them had any idea of who I was. That got me a small laugh from the audience. I decided to tell them a bit about my background, and my informal story was quite different from what the other nominees talked about. I recognised that my style was a risk, and I knew I didn't have much chance of being elected as vice-president. But I wasn't laughed off the stage, and I walked away feeling that I'd achieved what I wanted to. I wasn't elected to the vice-president's role. But I had challenged myself to speak in front of 800 people, and I achieved that. I also met a lot of people and expanded my networks.

23. Think realistically about time and effort: It's easy to forget that learning new things takes a lot of time and effort. You need to be ready to put in the hours, and the hours, and the hours. I hope you're not tired of my weightlifting analogies, because to me they're relevant. Getting good at weightlifting takes time – as I said previously, it takes at least three to five years to start to reach your full potential. But weightlifting also takes effort. Nearly every session is uncomfortable. You must be lifting weights that are challenging, otherwise you won't get stronger. When you lift a weight that's three times your bodyweight, it's extremely uncomfortable, and at first it doesn't feel safe. But the time and effort both happen in increments, and it's the increments that make it possible. By lifting a slightly heavier weight each week, eventually anyone can lift three times their own bodyweight. It's hard work, but it's achievable. Achieving at most things requires getting the balance of time and effort that works well for you. If you push too hard, you'll suffer some type of injury, stress, or burnout with possible long-term impacts on your physical or mental health. But if you don't push hard enough, you won't achieve your goal. Your task is to find your own Goldilocks zone, with just the right balance of time and effort to achieve the results you're seeking.

24. Take ownership over your attitude: Ultimately, your goals and your attitude are your choice. It's your life, and you're 100 per cent responsible for your choices. You can decide to set goals and work hard. You can also decide to spend your spare time watching tv or scrolling through social media. You're also responsible for your reactions to whatever

happens – you choose whether to keep going after a setback or whether to give in. You choose whether you approach each day with a positive mindset. You choose whether to get angry. You choose whether to replace negative thoughts with positive ones. Remember, you are in control of these choices. You can take ownership over your attitude.

If you cultivate a growth mindset, you're more likely to achieve the things you'd like to achieve. You're more likely to receive positive outcomes and live with the satisfaction of knowing you're doing the best you can. Having a growth mindset isn't always comfortable and it isn't always easy. But it's the best way to achieve long-term satisfaction and strong outcomes.

Plan Your Next Step

Have you thought about your next move? It's easy to get to a point in your career where you're ready for some sort of change, but you're not sure what the change should be. How do you make the change that's got the best chance of succeeding? Do you need to reinvent yourself?

People who are mid-career often feel ready to move up or move out, but they struggle to know how to make it happen.

Moving up

Let's think first about what it's like to move up within an organisation. It's easy to delay this – perhaps because the timing isn't right, or you think you're not quite ready, or you're worried about the consequences if you don't succeed.

I suggest that if you're thinking about moving up, then you're ready to give it a try. You'll never be 100 per cent prepared for a new role. So, if you're ready for a challenge and you think you're more than 75 per cent prepared, go for it.

If you're ambitious about moving up, then it makes sense to work ahead of your current position. Aim to understand the tasks done by someone one or two levels above you. And once you understand what's needed, aim to take on some of those tasks. If you're already doing some of the things required at that level, then moving up will be that little bit easier.

When you move up to the new position, keep looking forward. Once you're comfortable with the tasks required of you in this position, look two levels ahead once again. Keep challenging yourself to learn more and extend your skills and abilities.

Moving on

Of course, it's not always possible or feasible to move up within an organisation. Sometimes you need to move on. Perhaps you'll want to change organisations but keep working in the same field. And perhaps you'll decide to follow a new passion and try something completely different.

If you're nervous about making this type of change, try putting some perspective on your working life. If you're mid-career – say around 40 years of age – then you've probably been working for around 20 years – perhaps a bit longer if you consider the work experience you gained while you were studying. And you've probably got 25 to 30 years left in your career – perhaps longer if you love what you do. So, at 40, you've got a lot of your career ahead of you. If you're not doing the thing that makes you happy, you've got time to change.

If at 40 you decide to go back to university and study for a new career, you've still got time to have a challenging, satisfying career in your new discipline. The same applies at 50 or older: you can change careers and enjoy doing something different. You've got plenty of time.

Of course, for many people the decision is complicated by family responsibilities or a lifestyle you'd like to maintain. If you have a mortgage or school fees, then going back to university so you can swap careers might be a challenge. But a challenge doesn't make it impossible. You can decide what's most important to you and make the sacrifices necessary to achieve it. It's all about figuring out your priorities, then allocating the resources necessary to make the priority a reality.

If you're thinking of moving on and changing careers, think hard about why it's important and how you can make it happen. Don't complain about being unhappy then make a long list of excuses about why change isn't possible. Instead, find ways to set up a satisfying, long-term career. It might mean some short-term sacrifices, but they'll eventually be worth it.

Everything in Life Is a Trade-Off

Every decision you make about how to invest your time or your money involves some type of trade-off. You're choosing to invest in one thing, and trading in the opportunity to do or buy something else. By making one choice, you cut off the possibility of others. For me, this concept extends to everything in life. It applies to the house I choose to live in, the car I drive, the relationships I maintain, the friends I hang around with, and the way I choose to behave. It also applies to the things I achieve at work. Every choice opens things up in one direction but closes off something else.

It's easy to forget about trade-offs and choices. We assume that our decision to do something might have been the only option available to us. But that might not always be the case. You could have made different choices – ones that opened up your life in an entirely new direction. What we're talking about here is the opportunity cost of life – the multiple decisions that determine your life path and make you the person you are.

When you realise that everything in life is a trade-off, you can start to be more conscious about the choices you make.

Take time as an example. I often talk to people who say they can't do something or achieve something because they can't find the time. Often, it's something they claim they'd really like to achieve, but they're simply too busy to commit.

The reality is that everyone in the world has the same amount of time available to them each day. Each day has 24 hours in it, no matter who you are or where you live. Some people make choices that lead to them accomplishing things that are far beyond what other people think might be possible. Other people appear to achieve very little.

People who accomplish great things don't have more time, and often they don't have more skill. What they do have is focus. They set their sights on a goal they want to achieve, and they find the time to make it happen. They recognise that everything in life is a trade-off, and they trade away other choices to pursue their goal.

It's all about priorities

Next time you find yourself saying that you'd like to achieve something new or take on a challenge, but you're worried that you might not be able to find the time, I encourage you to stop and think. Reframe your internal monologue. Instead of saying, 'I don't have the time for that', try saying 'It's not a priority for me right now'. If, after giving it some thought, you decide that the idea really should be a priority, perhaps you'll be able to make the trade-offs necessary. If it's something you truly want, you'll be able to find the time to get it done.

Here's another thing to think about if you're running short of time. I suggest that you review the way you currently spend your downtime. Do you lose yourself in a television show or spend a lot of time on social media? If the answer is yes, then ask yourself whether that's the best trade-off you can make.

Maybe that relaxation time is important, and you don't want to give it away. But if you discover that you're spending 12 hours a week on social media while complaining that you don't have enough time to complete some beneficial training, maybe it's time to rethink the trade-offs you're making.

Make conscious decisions about the trade-offs you make in life and recognise that everything involves some type of trade-off. You may suddenly discover that you're able to achieve things you didn't think were possible.

Only You Can Define Your Success

Have you ever wondered about how you define success? Your definition of success may well be different from the definition of the people who work with you. If I lined up 100 people and asked every one of them to define success, I'd probably get 100 different approaches to the question. Yes, there would be themes and similarities, but everyone's definition would be slightly different. And that's because success is a highly personal, individual thing. Only you can define what success means for you.

To understand your definition of success, you need to know what you want out of life. You need to start by defining your goals and the things that bring you satisfaction.

Let's go back to the simplest definition: success is accomplishing an aim or purpose. Success isn't the pay-off – like the big mansion or a top-of-the-line luxury car. Instead, success is the achievement. It's accomplishing the aim or purpose.

Everyone has different aims and purposes in their life. Even family members have different aims and purposes. And that means, quite simply, that everyone will define success differently.

There's something important here about recognising the individual nature of success. It doesn't make sense to judge someone because their definition of success is different from yours. And it doesn't make sense for you to feel judged because your definition of success is different from that held by the people around you. You must live your own life, with your own definition of success.

Of course, society brings us challenges when it comes to defining success. If you look at the people who get public attention, you might get the impression that success means having an endless supply of money and living a life of fun – perhaps flying around on private jets, staying in mansions, and posing for social media posts. But it's highly likely that those images are giving you a false perception of what it means to feel successful and fulfilled. For most of us, posting images of ourselves in glamorous locations does not create deep feelings of success.

So instead of worrying about how society defines success, and instead of focusing on glossy images that don't provide any real insight into the person's life, focus on the things that you find fulfilling. What do you want to achieve? What does success look like for you? Perhaps it's having a career that's fulfilling. Perhaps it's being happy about going to work every day. Perhaps it's entirely focused on your family.

Make your own decisions

Remember that you're the one entitled to make decisions about what success looks like for you. Sometimes, your family might think they know what's best for you, but you're entitled to decide whether you agree.

I'll give you an example of a friend of mine, who works in the fitness industry. This friend is both driven and smart

– she could do whatever she wants, and she has chosen to work in the fitness industry. Her parents give her a hard time about her career choice, and often ask her when she's planning to get a 'real job'. That's tough for her to hear. What's a 'real job' anyway? One thing she's sure of – if she worked in an office job, which is probably what her parents mean by a 'real job', she wouldn't be happy at all. In the fitness industry, she's doing work she loves. And she's supporting her clients' physical and mental health. She finds her work personally fulfilling. She knows that she's a success, because she's doing work she's passionate about and she believes she's making a real difference for her clients. That's success, in her terms.

I hope that I remember this lesson when my son is old enough to think about his career. Finding purpose and fulfilment is much more important than pay or job security. I don't want my son to end up in a job that's not fulfilling, simply because he believes he needs the money. My son will live his own life, with his own definitions of success – which may well be very different from mine.

Aim for the Goldilocks zone

Having a fulfilling job doesn't necessarily mean that you have to accept poverty. Obviously, you can choose a job you like and still make a good living. The point is that the choice is the result of your interests, not the pay. If you're doing something you're passionate about and interested in, you're more likely to feel you're a success.

There's a book on this topic that I've enjoyed, called *Good to Great* by Jim Collins.[8] Collins uses a Venn diagram to help companies figure out what they do best, and you can apply

---

8. *Good to Great: Why Some Companies Make the Leap and Others Don't* by Jim Collins, 2001, Harper Business.

it at an individual level too. In the first circle of the Venn diagram, write down everything you enjoy doing and everything you think you would find fulfilling. In the second circle of the diagram, write down the skills you have that you're passionate about and those you think you can do better than most other people. Focus on the things you really care about and consider to be fulfilling. Then, in the third circle, write down the skills you have that you can make money from. Bring the circles together. What things exist in the overlaps? Is there something that exists in the intersection of all three circles? That's where you should focus your efforts – it's your own personal Goldilocks zone.

Think about what 'comfortable' means for you

Some years ago, I volunteered in high schools, teaching life skills courses. One of our sessions was about finances and budgeting, and I'd always ask the students what they'd like to achieve in terms of an income. Nearly every student said they wanted to be 'comfortable'. I used to ask everyone in the class to define what they meant by that – what exactly does it mean to be 'comfortable'? Most students would say that they wanted to be able to pay all their bills, put some money aside for savings, and have some money left over for entertainment. Most of them didn't want flashy things.

Then I'd ask them to imagine different scenarios, to get them thinking about how much money would be enough. I asked whether $100,000 earned by a couple would be enough. Most of the students agreed that it would be. Then I asked them whether $1 million would be enough. Well of course, they'd definitely be comfortable with $1 million.

Then I asked them to compare two options. The first option is to earn $100,000 per year, be able to pay all the bills, have some money for entertainment, and put away around 10 per cent as savings. The second option is to earn $1 million a year but with a lifestyle that requires you to spend every dollar you earn. You've got the latest and greatest of everything, but you never seem to have quite enough and you're not saving anything for the future. Most students decide they prefer the first option – they think the $100,000 lifestyle is a better example of living comfortably than the $1 million lifestyle.

It's a good lesson that we all need to remember. If your definition of success is to be comfortable, and if comfortable means managing with what you have, then increasing your pay packet isn't going to contribute greatly to your sense of success. Now, this isn't some idealistic stand against earning money. You need to earn enough to get by. But once you have that, getting more money isn't likely to help you feel more satisfied.

Remember that you're the only one who can define what success means for you. Do the things that bring you satisfaction and fulfilment. Focus on what this means for you, not what it means for others. That's the path towards feeling fulfilled.

Have Your Own Personal Value Proposition

Most organisations put a lot of time and effort into crafting their value proposition. It defines how they present the organisation to their target market. It helps the market to know what the organisation offers – what need it fills, what problem it solves, or what benefit it adds to people's lives.

If you think of yourself as your own personal product, then it makes sense to develop your personal value proposition. What do you offer to your target market? How do you position yourself? How do you want to be seen?

Your value proposition when you're looking for a new job

Let's imagine that you're on the hunt for a new job. You could be looking for a new job for all sorts of reasons – perhaps you're out of work, perhaps you're ready for a new challenge, or perhaps you'd prefer to work somewhere with a different culture. Whatever the reason, remember that you're applying for work in a competitive environment, and you need to find a way to stand out. That's where your personal value proposition comes in.

I've advertised mid-level roles that have received over 200 applications. And I've advertised for a senior executive and received nearly 100 applications from well-qualified, highly experienced, appointable candidates. In this environment, your application needs to stand out. A flashy CV is not enough.

When I'm reviewing applications, the ones that stand out are the ones that succinctly identify what the person offers and how they will benefit the organisation. They have a tight, clear personal value proposition. They catch my attention quickly; in one or two minutes, I know whether the application is worth reading more closely.

The written application needs to quickly capture the individual's personal value proposition and get the candidate to the interview stage. At the interview, the best applicants then present their personal value proposition verbally. They explain what they bring to the table – that is, what they offer the organisation and what their work will mean to the organisation. They don't just define their job title; they quickly capture how they approach the job. It's all about the value they bring.

Many job applicants list their previous job titles and qualifications. These things are important, but they don't help an applicant to stand out. Most of the people who apply will have roughly the same qualifications and years of experience. As a potential employer, I want to know what makes this person unique. I want to understand whether they'll fit with the team and add value to the organisation. And I make my judgement from their personal value proposition.

To develop your personal value proposition, examine your track record of success. Show what you achieved for each organisation. Quantify it if possible. For example, can you say that you contributed to your previous employer's profit by a set amount or implemented a change that saved a specific amount of money? Whatever is your equivalent of this type of quantification, look for it and then tell your story in a way that's clear, concrete, and accurate.

There's an example of this on my own CV. I was working in an organisation once and noticed a gap in leadership skills and ability. The organisation was full of technical experts but lacking in interpersonal skills and emotional intelligence. So, I developed a six-month leadership program to help senior managers develop these skills. I was able to measure its impact across the organisation. That example now sits in my CV to illustrate my ability to solve problems and innovate.

When you write your CV, focus on how to demonstrate the value you offer. Give real examples from your previous work and clearly state how those examples demonstrate your value.

Your value proposition when you want to advance in your current job

If you want to advance in your current role, having a clear understanding of your personal value proposition will help you to compete for a promotion or ask for a pay rise.

Within the workplace, your personal value proposition is the thing that sets you apart from your peers. It's your statement about the value you bring. This doesn't mean that you're putting down or discounting your colleagues; it just means that you've identified what you can offer.

To identify your personal value proposition, focus on the benefit you bring to the organisation, not your time in the job or the hours you work. It doesn't matter if you work harder than everyone else. It doesn't matter how much you currently earn. What matters is the value you bring and the evidence you have.

If at all possible, identify concrete details that demonstrate your effectiveness. Try to show exactly how much money you've saved or how much you've increased efficiencies. Gather numbers and data. Collect responses from people. Aim to provide objective evidence of your success.

Three tips on developing your personal value proposition

1. Quantify or qualify your achievements: If possible, break everything down into a dollar amount, ratio, or percentage. Describe any awards you've received. Quote statements of recognition. Show what you've done and explain how it goes above and beyond your current role.

2. Show how you solved a problem or achieved when the organisation would have otherwise failed: Explain the challenges faced by the organisation and how you helped to overcome them. Show times when you took on the hard jobs that no one else wanted. If possible, identify areas where the company is currently under-performing, and show how you intend to improve it.

3. Show how you're unique: Find something about you that's different from what might be expected of people with your skills and experience. Find something about you that's different.

Negotiating a pay rise or promotion

If you're negotiating a pay rise or promotion within your organisation, don't use another job offer as leverage. Don't negotiate by letting your employer know you've been offered more money to go elsewhere. If you want to stay in your current job, avoid using another job as a bargaining chip. It won't encourage your employer to trust you.

I have a firm rule with myself: if an employee uses another job as a bargaining chip, I tell them they need to take the other job. If the employee isn't happy working with me, then they need to go. I'm happy to negotiate with staff about pay rises and promotions, but only if they haven't applied for another job first. I believe that, by applying for another job and going through the interview process, the employee is showing they're no longer committed. And that means I don't want them in my team.

If you're seeking a pay rise or promotion, explain your justification as objectively as possible. Provide evidence to support your argument. This is most likely to be persuasive to your manager. Even if the promotion doesn't happen immediately, this approach is most likely to open the door for promotion in the future.

Be the Hero of Your Own Story

Do you want to be rich and famous? A lot of people chase this dream. But if it's the famous bit you're chasing, you might end up being disappointed.

If you chase fame, most likely you're trying to be a hero to everyone. You're yearning for recognition and appreciation. Instead, I suggest you aim to be a hero for yourself.

Be the hero of your own story, not anyone else's. If you're the hero of your own story, then you can be confident that you're doing the best you can for yourself and your family. You can achieve fame where it really matters – as respect from the people around you.

Focus on your local community

One useful way to extend the hero idea is to think about what it might mean to be a hero in your local community. How can you become someone who is well known in the community for all the right reasons? A community hero is someone the community can respect and trust – someone who has community spirit and integrity.

I guess that means there are two types of hero worth striving for. It's great to be the hero of your own story because you'll be living with self-respect and dignity. And it's worthwhile being a hero in your local community because you'll be contributing to the community in ways that benefit everyone. When you give to the local community – in whatever way makes sense for you – you'll find the community most likely gives back. Maybe you can coach a sports team or volunteer at the local school. Maybe you can serve on a community committee or council. And in return, you'll gain trust, respect, and friendship – a type of fame that really matters.

Don't chase rewards

If you focus on being the hero of your own story, you're likely to chase after things that matter – things that earn you long-term rewards like satisfaction and respect.

In contrast, if you chase rewards like fame, power, money, and glory, you're likely to focus on the pay-off rather than the task. The result will be a fleeting reward, or perhaps nothing at all. It doesn't make sense to chase rewards for the sake of the reward. Instead, chase the things that bring you satisfaction and learning, and the rewards are more likely to follow.

Be an inspiration to others

Another reason to focus on yourself and your community is that it will help you to grow into leadership. You'll become someone whom others can look up to and be confident in. If you live and behave like someone who inspires confidence and lives with integrity, you'll develop a reputation for those attributes in your community. That's one of the foundations for leadership.

There's no end goal

If you're the hero of your own story, you can focus on being the best you can be, every single day. That's where true satisfaction lies – with the internal rewards of knowing you're doing your best.

If you chase external rewards, like money and fame, you'll be stepping onto a treadmill that may never stop. How much fame is famous enough? How much money is money enough? The more you get, the more you'll want – and the more likely you'll end up disappointed.

Chasing money and fame is not likely to bring you long-term fulfilment. You may never find what you're looking for. Instead, recognise that there is no end point – no final goal when you can sit back and know you've made it. Focus on being the best version of yourself that you can be – become the hero of your own story – and that will set you on the path to true satisfaction.

There's No Such Thing as a Stress-Free Life

Social media posts often give the impression that the perfect life is a stress-free life. It's often perpetuated by a social media influencer who has something to sell.

It's garbage! There's no such thing as a stress-free life. And that's something to be grateful for.

Why would you want a stress-free life anyway? If your life was truly stress-free, then you would never develop resilience and strength. You wouldn't know how to handle relationships. You wouldn't know how to interact with your family. You wouldn't know how to bring up children. And you certainly wouldn't know how to handle money. It's not possible to live without stress.

It's all about finding the right level of stress

When it comes to stress, what really matters is getting it right. You need some stress, but not too much. Too little stress, and you're not really living. But too much stress, and it will begin to take its toll. And the amount of stress that's right for you is personal to you.

As you'd expect, it's a weightlifting analogy that comes to my mind. When I coach a new weightlifter, I aim to figure out just the right amount of stress for that person. I don't ask them to double the weights they lift within a week. Instead, I focus on incrementally increasing their weights each day. It's a small amount of regular stress that brings results – and the result is growth without injury. Small, regular stress brings longevity.

Focus on fine-tuning

In the weight room, we focus on fine-tuning the technical aspects of weightlifting. Tiny changes make a huge difference in terms of body stress. Then we invest in thousands and thousands of repetitions to build muscle memory. And every day or so, we add about 100 grams of weight.

Adding 100 grams of weight doesn't sound like much. But if you add 100 grams every day, then in 10 days you've added one kilogram. And that adds up. Theoretically in a year, you can add 30 or even 40 kilograms to your lifting – though obviously at some point you reach an upper level and the improvements start coming more slowly. But it takes three to five years of training to reach peak performance, and until then the gains can be pretty steady – providing, of course, you're balancing all the different aspects of fitness, like recovery, sleep, and nutrition.

The point here isn't about how much weight you can lift. It's about getting the level of stress just right. You need enough stress to encourage muscle growth, but not so much that it can't be sustained.

Balance stress, and seek help when it's needed

Let's apply a weightlifting analogy to life. You need enough stress to grow in your job, but not so much stress that it negatively affects your performance. You're not likely to go hunting for stressful situations at work, but you can be pretty much guaranteed that they'll appear.

When you encounter a stressful situation – whether it's at work or at home – the challenge is to monitor yourself. If it's too much for you to handle, then you need to seek support. Don't let yourself be broken by too much stress – just as you don't want to let yourself be broken by lifting too much weight in the weights room.

It's important to accept that there are times when professional support is vital. I'd like to share a bit of my own story to explain how important professional help can be.

About one year after my son James was born, when I was still living in the USA, I was struggling with severe depression and post-traumatic stress disorder (PTSD). I'd been deployed to Iraq and Afghanistan with the US Army and was being medically discharged after more than 18 years of service. I'd lost several friends and colleagues in Iraq and Afghanistan, and I was grieving for them. My army career was a huge part of my identity, and suddenly it was ending. I was losing the job I loved and the pride I felt in putting on my uniform every day. I felt used up and spat out.

Over a period of time, I convinced myself that the world would be a better place if I wasn't in it. I even wrote a letter to my family, explaining why they would be better off without me. Then one morning, when my wife and son went to the grocery store, I unlocked the front door and got myself organised. My plan was to ring 911 (the US emergency number), then end my life and let the emergency services find me before my wife got home.

When I picked up my phone to make the call, I flicked through some of my photographs and found a photo of two mates I'd served with – Napp and Knox – who had both died in Afghanistan. In that photo, they were both holding their babies – their babies were not that different in age to my son's age. One was born about a month before and the other about a month after. And that just got me thinking.

Napp and Knox had both had their lives cut short, and their babies were growing up without a father. Napp and Knox were great men who would have been able to teach their children a lot. They weren't given that choice. But for me it was a choice. And I knew I couldn't choose to leave my son. I owed it to my son and my wife to stay around. I had a responsibility to teach my son how to be a good man.

In that moment, I changed my mind. And I thank God every day for that. I learned to manage my depression and my PTSD with the help of some outstanding professionals. It hasn't been easy – and it's still not easy today. But it's so well worth it.

I guess that's when I truly realised that a stress-free life isn't a realistic goal. Sometimes life is hard. Sometimes life is stressful. But no matter what happens, you can make it through. And the world is a better place when you're in it.

If you're struggling, get some help. I can guarantee that it will be worth it.

Look After Yourself

I believe that everyone needs to develop a routine that gets their day off to a good start. It's not so much that any particular routine is right or best. What you need is a routine that works for you. I've established a strong routine that works for me, and it's something I follow every workday (and most non-workdays too). I'm sharing it here to show how important the routine is for me.

I'm an early riser. On workdays, I'm usually up at around 5:00 am. If I sleep in, I might get up at 5:30 or 6:00. I like to make the most of the early morning quiet for exercise and thinking time.

The first thing I do each morning is work out. I'm an avid weightlifter, and I like to keep fit. While the physical aspects of exercise are important for me, even more important is the time exercise gives me to clear my head and get ready for the day. If I'm feeling stressed about something or have some problem that I need to solve, it's usually while I'm lifting weights that things become clear.

I keep a small notebook close by when I'm lifting weights, and I use it to jot down things about the projects I'm working on. It's where I solve problems – and it's also where I outlined my last two books. While I'm lifting weights, I think. Then between sets, I make some notes in the notebook.

I also keep a whiteboard nearby when I'm lifting weights. There's something about the focus of weights that means it's the time when I'm most likely to come up with new ideas. I use the whiteboard to map out concepts and brainstorm possibilities. Together, the notebook and whiteboard help ensure that I don't waste the good ideas that float through my mind while I'm working out.

I'm fortunate to be able to work out alone. I've set up a home gym, and it allows me the luxury of being alone with my thoughts. But even in a crowded gym, you can lose yourself in what you're doing, shut off the noise around you, and use the workout time for generating new ideas.

Over the years, I've realised that I need quiet time by myself every day. It's critical for both my physical and mental fitness. I'm an introvert, and that time alone each morning is what makes it possible for me to work with large teams of people. I give myself about 90 minutes each day to work out and be completely alone. Those early morning workouts are my time because the rest of the day usually belongs to someone else.

At around 7:00 am, I shift to family time. We eat breakfast together and get ourselves organised for the day. Then at around 8:00 am, I'm on my way to the office. Again, I'm lucky – my office is around 10 minutes from my home, so I don't have a long commute to cope with.

As soon as I walk in the door of my office, my time is not my own. All day, I have demands on my time – with multiple meetings and people asking me to support whatever work they're trying to get done.

I'm rarely home before 6:00 in the evening, and sometimes it's later. Then it's back to family time, or sometimes I have social commitments or evening meetings. By the time I get to bed at night, usually between 9:00 and 10:00 pm, I'm both physically and mentally worn out. I often feel as though the demands of the day and the interactions with other people have sapped away all my energy. I need to recharge. I recover with a good night's sleep, knowing that I'll have my precious 90 minutes to myself the next morning.

Find time for yourself

I know that a lot of people find it hard to carve out some quiet time for themselves. But we all need time to relax and recharge. We also need time to think about how we're going – with our careers and our lives more broadly. If you don't find regular time for yourself, you might find that you lose sight of yourself as a person.

I strongly encourage you to establish a regular routine that works for you. It's not selfish to make time for yourself. No matter what level of leadership responsibility you hold, you need to find at least some time for yourself. And you need to do this regularly. It's absolutely essential. It's what you need to do if you're going to achieve at your best and feel confident about what you're doing.

For me, that time to myself is first thing in the morning, and it always involves working out. Maybe it's the same for you. Or maybe you need a different approach – at a different time of day and with a different activity that helps you focus. Whatever it is, make sure you do it. And when you figure out what your routine is, protect it carefully. It's one of the most valuable things you can do.

I know I'm repeating myself, but I need to reinforce that it's not selfish to make time for yourself. If you're in a leadership position, then your time is rarely your own. During the working day, you'll have almost constant demands on your time, and you'll need to be making decisions, considering options, discussing work strategies, and generally making sure things are operating as they need to.

And sometimes it seems as though your non-work time isn't yours either. You'll have family responsibilities or social commitments or community activities – or whatever it is that fills up your days. It's easy to slip into a pattern where you have no time for yourself.

If you're in the leadership game for the long haul, you need to find regular time that's just for you. You need time when you can think, reflect, and recover, without having any demands placed on you by other people.

Most days, I have a precious chunk of time when I'm only responsible to myself. I don't have to go anywhere. I don't have to interact with anyone. I can think about my life, my work, my relationships, and the things I'd like to achieve. I can also focus on keeping strong and fit – which to me seems like an essential part of coping with the other parts of life. It's absolutely essential for my personal wellbeing. Without it, I can't function well. That time alone helps to make me prepared for the day and ready to cope with whatever happens.

When I first started to carve out time for myself, I couldn't see how it was possible to find more than a few minutes in my day. So, I started with five minutes every morning. When I realised it was working well, I gradually built up the time. Now I aim for that 90 minutes to two hours, most days. My wife and my son both understand that I need that time to myself.

Maybe you don't need as much time alone as I do. What's important is to figure out how you can best support your own personal wellbeing, then invest time in making it happen.

Take time to think

One of the biggest challenges faced by leaders is the multiple conversations and meetings they're involved in every day. If you're listening to multiple ideas, conflicting perspectives, and complex concepts, you need time to think through those ideas and reflect. It's not possible to make good decisions without having some reflection time.

Try to make regular time in your diary for thinking and reflection. I read an article in *Harvard Business Review* titled 'How to Regain the Lost Art of Reflection' that suggested most executives need about two hours per week for thinking and reflection.[9] You might like to build that time into your diary. Make it a time when people know they're not welcome to contact you.

It's important for leaders to have some time every week when they can't be contacted. Ideally, this would be a few hours during the working week. But maybe it needs to be a weekend. Set aside a time when you don't respond to email and don't answer the phone. Make it a time when you don't send emails either, so you don't set up false expectations. Use this time to reflect on the decisions you need to make.

Avoid the weekend email trap

At one stage in my career, I used to put aside a few hours on Sundays to catch up on my email. These days, I don't check my email at all on Sundays. I've decided that I need to put aside that time for my family. I also realised that my Sunday email habit was causing stress for my staff.

---

9. 'How to Regain the Lost Art of Reflection' by Martin Reeves, Roselinde Torres, and Fabien Hassan, 25 September 2017, *Harvard Business Review* (https://hbr.org/2017/09/how-to-regain-the-lost-art-of-reflection).

If you're in a leadership position with staff reporting to you, it's likely that they'll feel compelled to respond to you if you email them on a weekend. You don't want to set up a pattern where you appear to be encouraging them to work on the weekend. Instead, do yourself and your staff a favour, and avoid sending work emails in non-work times. Obviously, there are exceptions for emergencies and crisis situations, but as a general principle, avoid weekend emails.

Make your personal time matter

When you're busy, it's possible that you'll give little attention to the things you do in your personal time because you're so focused on work. But you'll have a more balanced, satisfying life if you figure out what's important to you and make the most of the downtime you have available.

It's worth doing some personal financial planning and budgeting so you can make good decisions about how you use your money. With a bit of planning, you'll be able to decide what home tasks you need to do, and what you can outsource. You'll also be able to make good decisions about spending time with your family, or taking up some hobby that's always interested you.

The point here is to make sure that your downtime isn't just the time when you collapse with exhaustion. You want to make sure you have enough time to do the things that are important to you.

Don't expect all your happiness to come from work

There's a possibility that you, like most leaders, are highly invested in your job. Hopefully, it will bring you great satisfaction. It's also possible that you're doing a job you're passionate about, which is terrific. But job satisfaction and passion for your career are not everything. And it's important not to keep hunting for your 'passion job' while being miserable about everything else.

Mike Rowe, who hosts *Dirty Jobs* and several other shows, once said:[10]

> Stop looking for the right career and start looking for a job. Any job, forget about what you like. Focus on what's available. Get yourself hired, show up early, stay late, volunteer for the scud work. Become indispensable. You can always quit later and be no worse off than you are today. But don't waste another year looking for a career that doesn't exist. And most of all, stop worrying about your happiness. Happiness does not come from a job. It comes from knowing what you truly value and behaving in a way that's consistent with those beliefs.

It's important to remember that work might not make you happy, but it can make you content. Most people enjoy some things about their job, but not everything. And some people simply accept that their job is what they do to provide them with an income – and the income lets them build the life they want. This is ok. Not everyone needs a 'passion career'.

---

10. Mike Rowe is best known for his work on the Discovery Channel series *Dirty Jobs* and the CNN series *Somebody's Gotta Do It*. He has a podcast called *The Way I Heard It with Mike Rowe*.

What Is Resilience?

Resilience is a bit of a buzzword in business and in politics. We hear a lot of discussion about how we need to be more resilient as individuals, and how we need to develop resilient communities. We hear about resilient workforces. There's an increasing focus on how to build resilience in the face of uncertainty – whether that uncertainty is financial, social, environmental, or personal.

So, what does it actually mean to say we want to build resilience? Is there an end goal? How do we know when we have it? How can we become more resilient – both personally and in business?

Let's start with a definition. Resilience is the capacity to recover quickly from difficulties or tough times. It's about having a form of elasticity, which allows the object or person to spring back into shape after being exposed to a stress of some type. So, for individuals, resilience is having the capacity to bounce back after difficult times. It's about dealing with challenges and still holding your head high. It's about seeing beyond your current stress and coping with whatever life throws at you.

Stress is everywhere

Resilience and stress go hand in hand. And part of the rationale for building resilience is the simple fact that there's no such thing as a stress-free life (something I discussed in more detail in the chapter titled 'There's No Such Thing as a Stress-Free Life'). There's no easy life and it doesn't make sense to seek a stress-free life. No matter who you are, you will experience things that are stressful. Most likely, you will experience the death of a relative or close friend, and you will go through a mourning process. You're also highly likely to experience some type of financial stress – no matter what your financial circumstances are. And of course, most people experience some type of relationship stress and tension between family members.

The idea that stress is inevitable also extends to work. Everyone experiences stress of some type in their working life. You're likely to experience deadlines, work pressures, and constraints. You're likely to have your work limited by policy issues or economic issues. You're highly likely to experience conflicts of opinion and tensions over work practices.

The point here is to recognise that stress is inevitable, and it doesn't make sense to focus all our attention on avoiding it. Some level of stress is both helpful and necessary. Instead, it makes sense to focus on building resilience, so that you can deal with stress in the best possible way.

Resilience develops with practice

Resilience is one of those things that develops with practice. As you experience stress, you learn more about how to handle it and work through it – providing, of course, that the stress is something you can handle. Each stress you resolve builds your capacity to deal with the next thing that comes along.

The weightlifting analogy works well here. A weightlifter gets stronger by slowly increasing their weights. With each session in the gym, their muscles get a bit bigger and a bit stronger. Over time, they can build great strength. But if I asked a gym newbie to lift 100 kilograms, the result would probably be significant injury. It would be too much stress, too soon.

It's the same with workplace stress and any other stress you face in your life. Small, regular stresses help you to grow. They build your resilience and make you a stronger person. But too much stress can break you.

Don't be reluctant to seek help

It's important to remember that stress and resilience are both poorly defined concepts that are almost impossible to measure. Something that's a near-unmanageable stress for me may be an everyday occurrence for you. Our experiences of stress and our reactions to it are individual. Our capacities for resilience are also individual.

If you're struggling with excess stress or limited resilience, it makes sense to seek help. You might choose informal support from a trusted friend or colleague, or you might choose to seek more formal support from a therapist.

It's helpful to have trusted friends or colleagues you can open up to and get support from. They're the people you can unload with and get things off your chest. Having a strong network is one of the things that will help to build your resilience.

But if things get difficult, you may need more than your network of friends and colleagues. Don't be afraid to seek help from a trained psychologist or psychiatrist if you need professional support.

Resilience doesn't mean that things stay the same

Being resilient doesn't mean that you have the capacity to keep everything the same. And it doesn't mean that life will get back to how it was if you experience a major disruption.

Resilience can help you to bounce back or create a new way of being in the world – a new normal that accommodates your changing circumstance. After a major disruption, your perspective on things may change, and your new state of normal may be different from what it was before. Your ambitions may be different, or you may value different things. This is completely normal, and it doesn't mean that you're lacking in resilience. Far from it.

Relationships Are Powerful

Relationships matter a lot. They provide you with support, friendship, a source of advice, and the confidence to keep going. For leaders, all relationships are important – both professional and personal.

Professional relationships

Professional workplace relationships help you to achieve things. It makes sense to surround yourself with people who support you, who want you to achieve, and who can help you to look at situations objectively. You need to make sure that the people closest to you are genuinely there to support you: they're not 'yes' people who will agree with everything, and they're not nay-sayers who don't want you to achieve.

It's highly likely that your strongest professional relationships will be with a small group of people – your inner network of people who support each other to achieve. This is the group you're most accountable to and you'll learn the most from.

Outside your core group of professional relationships, you're likely to have a wider circle of looser professional relationships.

It's worth reflecting on whether the people in your core professional relationship group have goals, ambitions, and values that align with yours. You need to surround yourself with people who will support you – and with people whom you can support. A like-minded group can work together to achieve each individual's goals. Surround yourself with people who will push you forward in a positive way and will provide you with guidance when it's needed. Don't maintain relationships with people who seem intent on holding you back or who encourage you to question your goals.

Personal relationships

Personal relationships – with friends and family – provide you with a social network and an essential balance in your life. For an introvert like me, it makes sense to have a very small, strong group of personal relationships, plus a wider group of social contacts. For me, having a small core group helps to ensure that I feel supported and trusted, and that I can offer trust and support in return.

I don't believe that it's possible to maintain a personal relationship with 1,000 people or so. A big group might be a loose network, or maybe even a group of 'followers', but they're not people who are part of your core personal relationship group. Core relationships require your time, focus, and interest – something that most of us can only achieve with a small group.

Consciously choose your relationships

It's important to make conscious decisions about who you include in your core group of relationships – both professional and personal. Don't feel that someone needs to be in your core group simply because they've known you for a long time or because they're a member of your family.

Your core relationships need to support you to live the life you've chosen to live. Build relationships with people who support you and genuinely care for you. Ideally, your core relationships should be with people who will help you, and with people you want to help. If your relationships are strong, then providing support to others will add value to your life.

It's ok to cut off (or distance) relationships that are not working for you. You don't need to maintain relationships with people who are anxious to tell you what to do or who keep a tally of the favours owed to them. You don't need to maintain relationships with people who take advantage of you.

Think, too, about what you're offering. Make sure your relationships are not only about the help you need. If people only hear from you when you want something, they'll soon catch on and you might find they become distant. Remember that relationships involve both give and take – you can't expect to always take.

I read somewhere that each person is the sum of the five closest relationships they have.[11] Often, your five closest relationships will be with family members. You need those relationships to be supportive and positive, preferably with shared goals. If that's not your experience, then maybe something needs to change. Changing or forming new relationships is something I've struggled with – most likely because I'm an introvert. But it's something I have accomplished, and it's something you can accomplish too, if it's needed.

---

11. I don't remember where I read this, but motivational speaker Jim Rohn (1930–2009) is credited with suggesting that each person is the average of the five people they spend the most time with.

How to build new relationships

If your core group is too small, it's worth putting in some effort to build new relationships – whether professional or personal. Look around your networks for people who have achieved things you relate to and people who work in a way you admire. Don't be afraid to take the first step and introduce yourself to those people. Seek them out and learn from them. Building professional relationships is nearly the same as building personal relationships. They take time and are built on trust. Therefore, don't rush the relationship process.

As an introvert, I'm usually more comfortable choosing not to talk to people – particularly people I don't know. Being an introvert isn't the same as being shy. I'm far from shy and usually have no problem introducing myself to others. But I prefer to keep my thoughts to myself, and I usually prefer to focus on my own thoughts and ideas rather than on what's happening around me. I'm happy keeping my own company.

But I know that relationships are important, and I've developed strategies to overcome my reluctance to meet new people. One of these is that I set myself a goal to meet new people every time I attend an event or conference. I usually set quite a low goal – perhaps to meet two or three new people. With the goal in mind, it's easy to persuade myself to meet new people.

Another strategy comes into play if I know in advance that someone is attending an event that I'll also be attending. In this circumstance, I often connect with the person via LinkedIn, and send a message letting them know I'm looking forward to meeting them at the event. I find this method gives me a soft introduction and helps to break the ice prior to the event.

Quit Trying to Get People to Like You

When I'm talking to new leaders, one of the things that often comes up in conversation is that they want to feel liked. New leaders often want to know how they can get people within the workplace to like them. My answer is always the same: it's great to be likeable and it's great to be liked, but you must not focus on getting people to like you. Being liked isn't the goal.

As a leader, your goal is to make good decisions and work in a way that builds trust, confidence, and respect. You want people to believe you're doing the right thing. You want people to feel confident that implementing your decisions will take the organisation in the right direction. But you don't necessarily want people to like you. And you certainly shouldn't work hard to be liked – because that path could lead to compromise.

Interestingly, research suggests that successful leaders are usually well liked – so leadership and likeability do often go together. But being likeable and working hard to be liked are not the same thing.

You are not automatically right

Just because you disagree with someone, that doesn't mean you're automatically right and they're automatically wrong. And it shouldn't mean that your opinion prevails, simply because you're the leader. Great leaders understand that it's important to reflect on decisions. And sometimes you'll need to change your mind. Reflect honestly on feedback and suggestions, and if change is called for, feel confident enough to implement it.

You will not be liked by everyone

The reality of leadership is that you will not be liked by everyone. There are multiple personalities within every organisation, and it's not possible to get along with everyone. That's ok. Just because you don't much like someone, it doesn't mean you can't work together. Being liked should not be the basis of your working relationship. Instead, your working relationship should be based on things like trust, understanding, and confidence.

You don't have to like everyone you work with

Remember that likeability goes both ways: you don't have to like everyone you work with. In fact, it's probably not possible for you to like all your staff!

You don't have to like someone to get along with them at work. You can still be professional and still work together, without becoming good friends.

If you feel that you don't get on with someone who is part of your team, challenge yourself to reflect on whether this is hurting the workplace. Is it a simple case of a personality difference, or is there something bigger going on? Is the person doing their job well? Are they doing anything that's detrimental to the team? If it's just a simple personality difference, it's important that you find a way to work together. You can create a strong, stable team without personally liking everyone who is part of it.

Not everyone will like your decisions

Another reality of leadership is that some people won't like the decisions you make. Some people will dislike *all* of your decisions. Other people will appreciate some decisions but not others. And sometimes, people who don't like your decisions will feel very confident about sharing their opinion with their colleagues and with you. This is also ok.

You don't want to be working in a team where everyone always agrees with you. Those teams run a high risk of negative outcomes like groupthink.[12] Your job is to lead the team or organisation to the best of your ability, and to make decisions that reflect the widest interests possible. If someone doesn't agree with you, respect their disagreement. It makes sense to listen to their concerns and think about whether their points are valid. You may conclude that your decision needs to be refined.

If you have open lines of communication with your staff, people should feel welcome to give you feedback and question the decisions you're making. With open lines of communication, you'll also be able to explain why you're doing things and build trust that you've got their best interests at heart.

Remember that disagreeing with someone isn't the same as undermining them. If your team is willing to disagree with

---

12. Groupthink happens when a group reaches a consensus without careful reasoning or evaluation, often because no one wants to upset the rest of the group.

you, that's likely to be a sign of a strong, robust relationship and a healthy workplace. But if someone is trying to undermine your leadership, they're likely to be working against you in a toxic way. This is something you need to address.

Don't make popular decisions

As a leader, sometimes you'll need to make hard decisions. They won't always be popular. You need to have the courage to do what's best for the organisation, even if it's not the popular choice. Yes, people may be angry with you, but you still need to make the decision that's best. If you can communicate clearly about why you made the unpopular decision, you'll usually find that people will accept it.

If someone in your team expresses anger or resentment about a decision you've made, try not to react with emotion. Instead, try to understand what's really going on. Is the person genuinely concerned that you've made the wrong decision for the organisation? Or is it more of a personal response? Does the person have good reason to be emotional? What can you do to defuse the situation and help people understand why the decision was made?

Don't complain about the people you don't get along with

When you've got people in your team with whom you don't get along easily, remember that it's not ok to gossip or vent to other people at work. If you're a leader, you need to lead – and that includes not gossiping about other staff.

It's helpful to have someone you can share your problems and concerns with. But make sure you choose someone who is outside of your team – preferably a peer in a different organisation. They'll be able to listen to your concerns and encourage you to question whether you are thinking objectively without compromising anything that's happening within your team.

Don't let yourself be easily offended

Leaders need to make tough decisions, and those decisions won't be liked by everyone. All leaders experience challenges and difficulties within the workplace. Remember that, as a leader, it's your job to make decisions that serve the best interests of the organisation. If those decisions are unpopular, you may find that people within your team become upset. You need a thick skin. You mustn't let yourself get offended, simply because some people disagree with your decision. If you're easily offended, then leadership is not for you.

Quit Trying to Be Perfect

It's easy to fall into the trap of thinking you need to be perfect – or near-perfect – before you can take on responsibility or do a particular task. It's simply not true! You don't need to be achieving at a near-perfect level before participating in something – and that applies to pretty much everything in life.

I think that social media needs to take a lot of the blame for this trap. Social media presents us with endless images of seemingly perfect people achieving seemingly perfect things. They make it look so easy! Just remind yourself that you're looking at a façade. You have no idea what sits behind that façade, but you can pretty much guarantee it's not perfection.

You don't need to be 100 percent prepared before taking on new tasks. And you certainly don't need to be capable of doing every task at the highest level of competence.

You don't need a perfect plan

Here's an illustration of the trap of perfection as it relates to business plans. I've worked with a number of organisations that have put a huge amount of effort into planning. They plan, and plan, then plan some more, aiming to produce the perfect plan. They keep imagining scenarios and expanding the plan, so it addresses every possible option and every step of the process. They expect the plan to be the perfect blueprint for whatever they're hoping to achieve. And once the plan is done, they expect to follow it exactly, because it's a perfect plan.

But there's nothing realistic about aiming to write a perfect plan. As soon as you hit the implementation stage, things will change. A good plan gives you the flexibility to embrace that change, while a perfect plan might be a straitjacket.

So, quit trying to write a perfect plan. If you aim for the perfect plan, you'll fail – and you might end up doing nothing. Instead, write a realistic plan that incorporates some flexibility. Make sure the plan is good enough so you can get started. That's all it needs to be.

You don't need a perfect product

When you're developing a new product or service, it's tempting to remain at the development stage until the product is perfect. Of course, you want to respond to the needs of your customers and produce the best product you can. But instead of striving to produce a perfect product, it makes sense to come up with a minimum viable product, launch it, and then let it further develop as you understand its place in the market.

In the development phase, you're unlikely to understand exactly how your customers will use or respond to your product or service. That's why you need to build in some flexibility – and an ability to adapt as you learn more about customers' needs.

It's highly unlikely that your product will be perfect the day it's released. For that reason, it makes sense to start with a minimum viable product, then put your effort into further development over time. As long as you've got the basics in place, you can refine your offering as you go. You can put your money into learning from your customers and developing your product or service, so it fully responds to their feedback.

If you aim for perfection before entering the market, there's a good chance you'll fail.

You don't need to be a perfect fit for a job

If you're looking for a new job, remember that you don't have to be the perfect fit. You don't need to have every skill or attribute listed in the position description, and you don't need to have exactly the experience they describe. Don't stop yourself from applying for a new job simply because you don't have everything they've asked for.

Remember that no one is ever going to be a perfect fit for a job. Recruiters are looking for the best fit and the right attitude – and if you've got most of the attributes they're seeking, that might be enough.

You don't need to be perfect at every task

Don't stop yourself from applying for a job or taking on new responsibilities simply because you're not perfectly competent at every task required. Your competence will grow while you're in the job. You don't want to be perfectly competent before you start – otherwise there will be no challenge.

If you wait until you're perfect at every task before applying for a higher-level role, you will never get there. Sometimes, skills and competence can only be developed within a role. If you've got most of the skills and experience required, give it a go. You can soon learn any parts you're missing.

You don't need to be fit to exercise

It's incredible how often I hear people say they need to improve their fitness before they can join a gym or enrol in some exercise program. Yes, people really do think this, and it's even more crazy than thinking you need to be perfect at work.

The whole purpose of joining a gym, enrolling in an exercise program, or lifting weights is to improve your fitness or strength. If that's the purpose of the task, why would you need to make progress before you even begin?

Some people get worried they'll be embarrassed if they're a complete newbie who is weaker or less fit than everyone else. In reality, everyone in a gym is pretty much focused on achievement and progress, not the starting point. And most people will focus on their own progress, not yours. If you don't exercise, you'll never get fit. If you don't lift weights, you'll never get strong. And if you wait to get strong before you start, then you'll simply never start. You need to participate to make progress, and your starting point is irrelevant.

Aim for challenge, not perfection

Whether it's about work, fitness, or other aspects of your life, remember that you don't need to be perfect. Instead, you need to challenge yourself. Be willing to try things.

Don't be afraid to put yourself out there and accept a challenge. If you wait until you're fully ready for something, and if you constantly try to be perfect, you won't get very far.

Address Imposter Syndrome

Do you ever doubt your skills or your talents? Do you feel that your accomplishments are based on luck not hard work? Do you wonder whether people's compliments are true, and suspect that they're just trying to make you feel better? Do you worry that someone will uncover your carefully constructed public persona and discover that you're a fraud?

If any of this rings true, then you've experienced imposter syndrome. It's hugely common, and it's something you should work hard to address. It's not a helpful trait.

Imposter syndrome was first identified in 1978 by the psychologists Pauline Rose Clance and Suzanne Ament Imes.[13] Clance and Imes were the first to name imposter syndrome, but it's something that's been around for a very long time. And it's not going anywhere. In 2011, an article in the *International Journal of Behavioral Science* suggested that more than 70 per cent of people experience imposter syndrome at

---

13. 'The Imposter Phenomenon in High Achieving Women: Dynamics and Therapeutic Intervention' by Pauline Rose Clance and Suzanne Ament Imes, 1978, *Psychotherapy: Theory, Research and Practice*, Vol. 15, No. 3, pp. 241–247.

some point in their career.[14] It's one of those things that many people experience, and few people like to admit.

One of the biggest challenges with imposter syndrome is that it encourages people to assume their successes are due to luck, while their failures are a true reflection of their ability. This is a recipe for giving up – or, at the very least, not bothering to put any effort into career development. If success is luck, then what's the point in trying? Imposter syndrome can also lead to other problems, like excess anxiety, stress, and depression.

Research suggests that women are more likely to experience imposter syndrome than men. I haven't found a lot of literature about why this happens, but it's a well-established gender difference.[15]

Imposter syndrome happens in all aspects of life. It's not confined to work – many people also experience imposter syndrome in their personal relationships or with their hobbies. At home, imposter syndrome may be the result of feeling that you're not living up to the expectations of your partner or other members of your family. You may be more likely to experience imposter syndrome if you had over-protective parents, a family trait of perfectionism, or if you suffer from low self-esteem or excessive self-monitoring.

Imposter syndrome is not helpful. When you notice it in yourself or others, it's important to call it out and challenge it. I've got five ideas to help overcome imposter syndrome.

---

14. 'The Imposter Phenomenon' by Jaruwan Sakulku and James Alexander, 2011, *International Journal of Behavioral Science*, Vol. 6, No. 1, pp. 75–97.

15. See, for example, the article 'Women More Likely to Suffer from Imposter Syndrome than Men, According to Research' by Oliver Lewis, 7 April 2023, *The Independent* (https://www.independent.co.uk/life-style/women-imposter-syndrome-workplace-confidence-b2313770.html).

1. Recognise that you're not alone: The first challenge is to recognise what imposter syndrome is, recognise that it's not a helpful thought pattern, and recognise that it's common. You are not the only one who feels this way. Lots of people feel like an imposter, and most people are not brave enough to admit it.

2. Learn about it: Once you recognise that you're not alone, you can arm yourself with knowledge about how imposter syndrome works. Read about it and, better still, talk to colleagues and friends who have experienced it. Share your experiences. Find out how other people have addressed it. You may be able to help each other.

3. Remove self-doubt and build confidence in your abilities: Monitor yourself and watch out for those times when you start to question your abilities. Remember that you are in control of your thought processes, and you have the ability to stop doubting yourself. When you find yourself struggling with self-doubt, spend some time focusing on the skills and experience you've already accumulated. Remind yourself that your achievements are not simply due to luck.

4. Keep learning and improving: The best way to challenge imposter syndrome is to deepen your knowledge and confidence. Whenever you feel as though you're lacking in skills and experience, focus on how you can change that feeling. What do you need to learn, or do, or practise so you no longer feel like an imposter?

5. Remember that you don't have to be perfect to be right: One of the biggest contributors to imposter syndrome is the sense that everything has to

be perfect. If it's not perfect, then you must be an imposter – right? Well, no, actually. Perfection doesn't happen very often. And to get things done or make the right decision, you don't have to be perfect. You just need to be good enough.

Watch out for imposter syndrome in yourself and others. When you see it, call it out. Name it. Challenge it. And work hard to get over it. Imposter syndrome is not a reflection of reality. And it will hold you back.

Watch Out for Unconscious Bias

Unconscious bias is one of those leadership traps that can only be managed with constant vigilance.

Here's a quick definition: unconscious bias (or cognitive bias, as it's sometimes known) is a basic misstep in thinking, assessing, or recollecting. It's a flaw in your thinking that you're not aware of. It's a type of shortcut – but it's a shortcut that encourages you to accept some decisions or people and reject others.

There are many, many types of unconscious bias. Several articles list at least 50 different types.[16] And everyone exhibits at least some of them.

Unconscious bias leads us to process information in a particular way. It influences how we interpret situations, how we assess people, and how we react. It's simply a condition of being human.

Unconscious bias can help us to make decisions quickly and help us to make predictions in any situation. This is useful when we're making complex decisions. The trouble

---

16. See the Wikipedia entry at https://en.wikipedia.org/wiki/List_of_cognitive_biases.

is that unconscious bias can encourage us to make decisions based on flawed logic or unsound reasoning.

Bias blind spot

I read an article some time ago called 'Bias Blind Spot'.[17] In the article, the authors comment that a 'lack of conscious access to judgment-forming processes means that people are often unaware of their own biases … even though they can readily spot the same biases in the judgments of others'. The authors note that most people believe they are less biased than their peers – in both their judgement and their behaviour.

So not only do we all have unconscious bias, we also have a bias that makes us think we're each less biased than the people around us! It's easier to notice biases in other people than it is to notice biases in ourselves. We have what the authors call a 'bias blind spot'.

The article's authors suggest that the bias blind spot comes from the interplay of two other phenomena – the introspection illusion and naïve realism. The introspection illusion leads us to believe that our own introspections are unbiased – that is, that we reflect on our own feelings, emotions, and mental state in an unbiased way. Naïve realism is a belief that our own perception of the world reflects the true state of the world – that our assessments are genuine, not biased. We all suffer from the introspection illusion and naïve realism – and when they're put together, we end up with a bias blind spot. We assume that everyone sees the world the way that we do. We forget that everyone's perspective is unique.

---

17. 'Bias Blind Spot: Structure, Measurement, and Consequences' by Irene Scopelliti and others, 2015, *Management Science*, Vol. 61, No. 10, pp. 2281–2547 (https://pubsonline.informs.org/doi/10.1287/mnsc.2014.2096).

Some of the most common biases

Here are some of the most common biases that tend to affect leaders. By becoming aware of them and watching out for them, you'll be able to challenge the ways you make decisions.

- Anchoring bias means that we tend to over-rely on the first piece of information we receive about a topic. When we're learning something new, we tend to hang on to the first piece of information we receive and use it to judge all subsequent information.

- Bandwagon effect is when we go along with an idea or a belief because many others seem to believe it. Most people find it difficult to disagree with something if everyone around them has already stated their agreement. It's difficult to go against the majority.

- Patternicity (also known as the gambler's fallacy) means that we tend to look for meaningful patterns in random data. It's tempting to look at random data and assume there's a pattern going on – and that the pattern may help you predict what will happen next. Patternicity is a fallacy.

- Confirmation bias means that we pay more attention to information that reinforces what we already believe and ignore information that's contrary. Often, we do this without even realising it's happening. We simply disregard something because it's not credible or not believable, without realising that our own confirmation bias is at play.

- Attribution error (also called attribution bias) is when people try to uncover an explanation behind their own or others' behaviour by over-estimating personal factors and under-estimating situational factors. A good example of this is when someone comes in late to a meeting, and you assume they're late because they're unmotivated or lazy. You don't take into account all the situational factors that may have made them late.

- Halo effect and bias-the-horn effect is when we judge people the same way on all traits – assuming that one person is good at everything (for the halo effect) or assuming someone is bad at everything (for the bias-the-horn effect). We end up assuming that people are either angels or devils and ignore all the space in between. The halo effect stops us from making a fair assessment.
- The ostrich effect means that we ignore or avoid bad news or bad data. If you're not willing to address the things that are going wrong, you may be suffering from the ostrich effect.
- Recency bias means that we remember what happened to us most recently and rely on recent things more than we should. We forget about previous experiences and rely on our most recent experiences to make decisions.
- Zero-risk bias is when we prefer a choice that provides a small risk with a smaller benefit, instead of something with a greater risk and much greater benefit. It's more tempting to choose the smallest risk, even when it's not the best choice.

Reflect on how biases might affect you

It's worth reading about and reflecting on the unconscious biases that affect us all. Becoming more aware of unconscious bias in the workplace will help you be more effective as a leader. Most importantly, being aware of unconscious bias will help to ensure you're careful about who you choose to employ and promote. If you're aware that bias is a possibility, you'll be more likely to avoid favouritism, choose the best person for each role, and bring diversity into the team. Reducing bias should also help to improve your team's decision-making, improve creativity, enable your team to consider a wider variety of options, and help your team to feel more positive about the workplace.

Addressing unconscious bias is an ongoing challenge. It's not something you can read about, learn, and then be done with. It's not something you can solve. Instead, you need to constantly challenge your human tendency for bias.

Challenging your own biases

Most people are blind when it comes to their own biases. One useful tool is the Harvard Implicit Assessment Test, which is available online through Project Implicit.[18] You can take their online test to help you understand your attitudes, stereotypes, and hidden biases.

A less formal way to look for your own biases is to be aware of the clues people give you in their feedback. If people make comments like 'you probably didn't think about this' or if you notice that your assumptions are different from those of others, you may want to examine whether an unconscious bias is the cause.

A practical way to challenge your own biases is to deliberately employ a diverse work team. If you welcome diversity

---

18. Project Implicit was founded in 1998 by Dr Tony Greenwald from the University of Washington, Dr Mahzarin Banaji from Harvard University and Dr Brian Nosek from the University of Virginia. See https://implicit.harvard.edu/implicit/.

and provide opportunities for people to contribute, you'll challenge your own unconscious biases.

Finally, consider implementing some formal training or discussion about unconscious bias in the workplace. This is an issue you need everyone to address. Encourage everyone in your team to become more self-aware and to have frank conversations about biases. It's not possible to remove unconscious biases, but you can become aware of them and address them.

Cultivate Moral Courage

Moral courage relates to the reasons why you choose to take action. It's about doing things because they're right, not because they're easy.

When you cultivate moral courage, you're able to take action because you know it's morally right, despite the risk of adverse consequences. Moral courage means you make decisions and take action even when you may suffer as a result.

Strong leaders cultivate moral courage, both for themselves and their team. They value and promote the responsibility that we all have to make decisions and take actions because they're the right thing to do. They lead by example. They know that moral courage requires careful thought and deliberation – that it involves working towards the greater good.

A simple example of moral courage at work

A simple example of moral courage can illustrate the point – such as a team member's decision to help someone, even if that decision makes the workday more challenging.

Imagine you're driving to work one morning, with your eye on the clock because you've got an important appointment coming up. As you're driving along, you notice there's a vehicle pulled over on the side of the road, with a driver who's struggling to change a flat tyre. For you, changing a tyre is easy. But if you stop and help, you'll run the risk of being late for your appointment. Do you stop and help? Or do you get to work on time and hope someone else stops to help? Or do you just leave the person to struggle alone with their tyre, because it's not your problem?

If you're a person with moral courage, you'll stop and help with the tyre, while quickly letting your colleagues know you might be late. If your workplace is flexible, accommodating, and the type of place that encourages moral courage, then the decision is easier. You can simply explain what's happening, and the people you're meeting with will be likely to understand.

Of course, there's another aspect to this simple story of moral courage. If you pull over and help the driver, you'll not only be late for work; you'll also face the risk that comes with changing a tyre on the side of a road. Yes, it adds another dimension of risk to the situation, but most people would still argue that the morally right thing to do is to stop and help.

As a leader, you can cultivate moral courage within your team by demonstrating it in practice and celebrating it when it happens. As an emerging leader, you can set an expectation for moral courage by demonstrating its value. Show moral courage. But, at the same time, communicate with your colleagues to minimise the chances of misunderstanding or confusion.

Moral courage in the face of bullies

Here's a riskier example of moral courage: calling out a bully. If you're working in an environment where your supervisor is a bully, how can you cultivate moral courage? Is the best approach to call them out or to look for another job?

A strong leader will, of course, call out the bully. It needs to be done professionally, and it needs to be done in private. Even bullies need to be treated with dignity and respect. But the courageous aspect of this situation is that no matter how professional and respectful you are, your actions could lead to serious repercussions. The bully could make your working life even more difficult than it currently is. And you could get fired.

In the face of a bully whom you work for, you need to decide which approach is best for you, given the context you're in, the difficulties caused by the bully, the extent of your moral courage, and the risk of negative repercussions.

I've faced this situation, and I decided to risk losing my job. I decided that the bully needed to be addressed. And if addressing it meant that I was going to lose my job, then that was a risk I was willing to take. To be honest, if the culture of the workplace is one that allows a bully to thrive, then it's not the right place for me to be working anyway. Either I deal with the culture, or I need to move on.

In the situation I found myself in, I organised a meeting with the bully and explained why I believed their actions were inappropriate. This person acknowledged their behaviour but brushed it off as 'that's just the way things are' and said that things weren't going to change. I left the organisation shortly after. And after a few more staff left due to the behaviour of the bully, the organisation eventually asked the person to leave.

Of course, the decision to leave or risk losing your job might not be straightforward if you're working in a context where another job won't be easy to find, or if you've got workplace relationships that you value and don't want to lose.

Moral courage in the face of wrongdoing

Here's another situation where moral courage is relevant. Imagine you become aware that someone is intentionally doing the wrong thing in the workplace – perhaps some type of fraud or some other illegal activity. How does moral courage apply here, particularly if the perpetrator is a friend?

In the face of wrongdoing, you have a responsibility to act. If you are aware of a problem – no matter what that problem is – and you do nothing about it, then you're condoning the behaviour. If you fail to act, you become complicit in whatever is happening, and that's not a way to build a solid foundation in leadership.

Leadership requires moral courage

Moral courage comes into play whenever you are faced with an ethical choice or dilemma. Strong leaders demonstrate moral courage through their decision-making and actions. When you accept leadership responsibilities, the decisions requiring moral courage become tougher and more frequent. And whether you demonstrate moral courage will influence your stability as a leader and the faith and trust your people place in you.

Any time you fail to demonstrate moral courage, your team members will notice. You'll become known as a person 'without a backbone'. That's detrimental to the culture of your organisation, to people's perception of you as a leader, and to your longer-term abilities to lead.

Leadership isn't just about making people feel good and motivating them to do their best. It's also about making the tough decisions that must be made. It's about having the moral courage to make the right decisions and show everyone how to do the right thing.

Use Your Authority Responsibly

Leadership involves a level of responsibility and authority. Good leaders display natural authority, no matter how senior they are in an organisation. Leaders employed in senior positions also carry operational authority relevant to their role.

As a leader, you need to understand the authority you have and use it responsibly. The best leaders carry authority because their team willingly accepts it – the authority is something the leader deserves, not something they take or demand.

Can a leader show disrespect?

When I was serving in the US Army, someone told me that people in positions of authority can't disrespect their juniors. This was a neat way of saying that people who have been granted organisational authority can treat their subordinates any way they want. This person believed it wasn't possible to disrespect subordinates because subordinates don't deserve respect in the first place.

This view suggests that subordinates must respect their superior, but respect does not go both ways. It's a view that reflects – in my opinion – an irresponsible use of authority.

As you'd expect, this comment came from a leader who demanded authority but did not deserve it. Today, I recognise him as a bully.

Yes, a leader can show disrespect – and it's something that effective leaders actively work against. Effective leaders treat everyone with dignity and respect – regardless of the person's position in the organisation. They show respect because it's the right thing to do.

Avoid issuing instructions

A leader who uses their authority responsibly usually asks people to do things. They don't need to issue instructions because their team is happy to do what they're asked. Of course, the leader has the organisational authority to demand that various tasks are completed – and they'll do that if necessary. But a leader who understands how to use their authority responsibly will recognise that they're much more likely to get the job done well if they create an environment where people want to do what they're asked.

The reality is that, for many leaders, asking people to do things has the same effect as issuing an order. If you're in a position of authority within the organisation, your team will do what you ask – whether you ask pleasantly or issue an abrupt order. But the pleasant question is so much more friendly! And it will be more effective in the long term.

It's difficult for people to say no

There's an important implication of this idea that team members are likely to do what their leader asks. When a person in a position of authority requests something, it's difficult for most team members to say no. Many staff members believe they're not in a position to say no – even if they would prefer to. The leader's position of authority requires the team to do what is asked.

It's important for leaders to keep this in mind. If you hold a position of organisational authority, it doesn't really matter whether you phrase something as a gentle question or an instruction. The effect will be the same. And this means you need to be sure your requests are fair, ethical, and reasonable. You should never put a team member in a position of feeling compromised or conflicted by your requests.

I worked in an organisation once where a very senior member of the team asked a junior staff member to do something unethical. The junior staffer was concerned that, if they refused, they would either be reprimanded or lose their job. I was working in a different team, and the junior staffer came to speak to me about the problem. I was able to become an intermediary between the two people. What interested me most was that the senior staff member said they'd made a request, not a demand, and the junior staffer could have refused the request. The senior staff member had no idea about the difficult position they'd created. They forgot about the power imbalance between them.

This situation reinforced my belief that senior executives need to take great care to never put a person in a position where they feel forced to do something that might compromise their integrity.

Sometimes there may be ethical grey areas – where something might be problematic when viewed from a particular perspective. As a leader, it's your job to make decisions and show responsibility. Junior staff should never need to question your integrity. Never put junior staff in a position where they feel they need to choose.

Cultivate openness and transparency

Effective leaders develop a culture of openness and transparency. They're the type of leaders that people feel they can trust.

If you cultivate true openness and transparency, your team will never need to question your intentions or motivations. They won't be stuck in some sort of ethical dilemma, and they won't question what you consider to be right.

One of the biggest benefits of openness and transparency is that it creates a culture where staff feel able to ask questions about how decisions are made or why one approach is the best. If they trust the leader's intentions and ethics, they'll feel confident about asking questions that help them understand decisions.

The only way to build a culture of openness and transparency is to demonstrate that it exists. Your staff need to see the way you make decisions and feel welcome to ask questions. You can't just tell people that you're responsible and ethical. You need to demonstrate it consistently.

Remember that it only takes one slip – one occasion where you demonstrate poor ethics or ask someone to compromise their integrity – and you will lose all credibility. Building trust and credibility is slow and incremental. Losing it takes just a moment.

Never Say: 'That's Not My Job'

If you listen to conversations around any workplace, there's often a familiar theme. You'll hear people saying, 'that's not my job', or 'that's not in my position description', or maybe even 'that's beyond my pay scale'. If you're aiming for a leadership position, that's a theme you should seek to avoid.

For a start, remember that a position description is nothing more than an overview of what your job entails. It's not a detailed list of everything you'll be doing every day. If you work only to your position description, you'll be limiting yourself. You'll be forcing yourself into a type of straitjacket that makes it impossible to grow, learn, and respond to new opportunities.

It's important to recognise that any position description will evolve over time. If it doesn't, and if you stay in the same job for several years, you're not really getting an opportunity to learn and develop. If you have 10 years working in the same job with the same tasks, you don't really have 10 years of experience; instead, you have one year of experience, 10 times over. No matter what job you're doing, you should look for opportunities to let it evolve and grow.

If you get a reputation of avoiding things that are 'not your job', you're likely to be marginalised in the workplace. You may find yourself pushed aside, given only the tasks that fit within the tightly defined parameters of your job. You'll never go anywhere. But if your goal is to rise up through an organisation, then everything should hold your interest and many things should be your job. That's the way you show leadership potential and gain trust.

Everything is your job

When you take on a leadership position, everything becomes your job. Leaders don't have a set task list that they don't step outside. For leaders, any task that comes into the organisation is, in some way, their responsibility. They may not actually do the work, but they're the ones responsible for making sure it's done right. If a leader doesn't have the skills or resources to complete whatever task appears on their desk, it's up to them to figure out how to make it happen.

In any organisation, there will be tasks that appear – seemingly out of nowhere – which seem unsolvable or particularly challenging. Sometimes it's not clear which part of the organisation should take responsibility for a new task. If you've got leadership ambitions, then you should be willing to take on this type of task. Don't be daunted by its novelty or complexity. Don't be concerned if you initially have no idea how to approach it. Instead, be honest with your supervisor. Explain the challenges, discuss the support you'll need, and figure out a way of getting the job done. Show that you're capable of taking on the task and learning along the way. This may just be the opportunity you've been waiting for.

I suggest that any aspiring leader should be willing to take on pretty much any task – providing, of course, that it's legal, ethical, and moral. If you believe that it isn't legal, ethical, or moral, then you have the right to challenge the task and explain your concerns. Regardless of the relationship between you and your supervisor, or the potential for career progression, you should never take on a task that you believe sits outside the boundaries of the law or the community's ethical or moral framework.

If you have leadership aspirations, put your hand up for the difficult tasks. Let your supervisor know that you want to be challenged. Take every opportunity to learn new skills. As you demonstrate your success, you'll be able to move up within the organisation.

SECTION TWO

Leading Teams and Organisations

More than likely, in your first leadership role you'll be responsible for looking after a team. The team may be small or large, depending on things like the size and type of organisation or the style of work your team performs.

Whatever type of team you lead, one important concept to consider is your span of control. Span of control is simply the number of people, tasks, or events that you can effectively manage. Your effective span of control will be influenced by many factors – including the geographical dispersion of your team, the team's capability, your capability, and the types of tasks everyone needs to complete.

Some theorists have tried to quantify the optimal span of control, with many researchers suggesting that a team size of between three and seven people works in most organisations – though it's likely to be larger in a factory environment. Some theorists suggest that five is the optimal size for a team in many office environments.[19]

If the number of people in your team grows too much, you'll be less effective as a leader. When this happens, it

---

19. Wikipedia has a detailed entry on span of control.

makes sense to either split teams or add a new layer to the organisational hierarchy – both approaches can effectively reduce each leader's span of control.

Some leaders are stretched by the number of tasks they're expected to manage, rather than by the size of their team. If this happens, delegating is likely to become the best option.

This section of the book focuses on how you interact with your team, not on the technical aspects of team leadership (like delegating or managing projects). I'm particularly interested in two aspects of team leadership: how you communicate with your team and how you can best support your team to achieve their best.

As you move up the corporate ladder, at some point you'll hopefully end up at the top. Of course, I recognise that not everyone has this goal. But for those who do, you'll have a climb ahead of you – perhaps a short climb, or perhaps a very long climb that takes years to achieve. There's no one journey and no best way. Everyone achieves things at different rates, and everyone's context is different. Your task is to follow your own path.

This section doesn't focus on the practical aspects of leading teams and running organisations – such as reading a financial statement or developing a strategic plan. Instead, in this section I focus on your mindset, and how you can develop a way of thinking that will help you on your leadership journey.

Providing leadership for your team will always be important, no matter where you find yourself within an organisation's hierarchy. When you're leading an organisation in a senior position, your closest team is usually your direct reports – perhaps the senior leadership group within the organisation. By leading this team effectively, you can lead the whole organisation effectively through a pyramid effect. If you provide good leadership to the team closest to you, you'll encourage them to provide good leadership to their own teams.

Good leadership resonates throughout an organisation, and it starts at the top.

4 Steps to Building Your Tribe

'Building your tribe' is a current catchphrase in the business world. It was popularised in Seth Godin's book *Tribes: We Need You to Lead Us*. Try searching for it online, and you'll find a seemingly endless number of podcasts, books, blog posts, and online tips about why and how you should build your tribe. The aspect of tribe building that most interests me is the idea of building a personal tribe – a small group of people committed to supporting you and your work.

The idea of a personal tribe is pretty simple. It's about building a community around you or having a cohesive team who respect you and believe in what you're doing. It includes aspects of developing an informal following – of being surrounded by people who support you in what you're trying to achieve or help with the movement you're trying to start. It's about being connected to a group of people who want to see you succeed.

It's that final concept that's most important: your tribe wants you to succeed. They're loyal and supportive. They'll help you make your vision into a reality.

Of course, the tribe concept can apply to anything. It makes sense in the workplace or in a new business. But it can also be applied to a cohesive sporting team, or a political party, or a religious group. And of course, the tribe concept can easily be applied to conspiracy theorists and hate groups. It's all about wanting to support or follow a particular person or movement – about being aligned to it or being part of it.

When it comes to thinking about your own personal tribe, what matters is that it's a supportive group with your best interests at heart. If your tribe provides you with the support and motivation you need, it doesn't matter whether it's large or small. A small, strong, cohesive tribe can help you to achieve strong outcomes and be a great source of collaboration and idea sharing.

Like attracts like

Building a tribe is based on the simple principle that like attracts like. Your personal tribe is highly likely to include people who share relevant interests and concerns with you – all focused on whatever it is that your tribe is there to achieve.

I've identified four important steps in building a personal tribe:

1. Understand who you are at your core: If you understand your own values and your motivations for wanting a group of people around you, you'll be better able to understand what you're trying to achieve and what types of support you need.

2. Be genuine: Be open with people about your motivations for building this group, your values, and what you hope to achieve. If you're not genuine, people will quickly see through you and take steps to dissociate themselves from you.

3. Be consistent: Make sure that what you say is consistent with what you do. At the same time, be

consistent in the way you voice your opinions, and display your values and principles. Don't change your views in an effort to appeal to everyone you meet.

4. Be loyal to those who follow you: You become a leader when someone chooses to follow you. When someone has displayed the trust and courage to align themselves with you, make sure you respect them and value them.

Don't aim to be everything to everyone

Remember that your tribe isn't going to be for everyone. You can't appeal to everyone you meet. And some people who genuinely support you won't have the time or interest to be part of your tribe. Focus on finding the people who believe in what you're doing, share your values, and are committed to working with you to achieve your goals. Your core group may be very small.

Building a tribe takes time. You need to develop a detailed understanding of what you're trying to achieve. You also need to devote time and effort to developing a sense of trust around you and building relationships with people who want to align themselves with what you're doing. If you want to build a tribe, you need to commit yourself for the long term.

Are You Leading or Managing?

When you employ someone to work in your team, you're usually employing someone who is experienced, well-educated, and smart. You need to recognise their skills and experience and give them opportunities to flourish. The more experience they bring, the more you need to focus on leading instead of managing.

Competent, experienced staff don't need to be told what to do and how to do it. Instead, they need strong leadership that motivates them to work to the best of their abilities.

Challenge yourself

If you find yourself closely monitoring work and explaining the way tasks should be completed, I suggest that you challenge yourself in two ways:

1. Have you got the right person in the right job? Examine the person's skills and capabilities, and question whether they are truly up to the task they've been employed to do. If they're lacking some competency, then training might be needed. But if they're clearly competent in their role, then maybe the problem sits with you.

2. Is your leadership style appropriate? Examine your approach and consider whether you're over-managing when it's not needed. Maybe you are standing in the way of success, and the best thing you can do is step back. Make sure you're a leader, not a manager. Give your staff the freedom they need to do the work you employed them to do.

Adapt your style based on their experience

Different staff will need different approaches to leadership and management. An effective leader is able to adjust their style to provide the right level of support for different staff.

New or inexperienced staff need close management, at least initially. They'll need guidance and direction about how to work effectively within the organisation. They may need training and they're likely to need a lot of support.

But as staff gain experience, you should be able to reduce your management and prioritise leadership. Experienced staff don't need a lot of guidance or close management. For experienced staff, close management will simply create frustration and discontent.

The challenge for you as a leader is to understand the support needs of each staff member and adjust your style accordingly. Provide management only if it's needed.

Focusing on leadership not management

Leadership is based in your organisation's vision, and a good leader motivates staff to work collaboratively, towards that vision. Your task as a leader is to provide the right environment for staff to flourish.

Some of the practical ways you can help staff to develop their skills and experience include:

1. Job rotation: You may be able to give staff an opportunity to move around the organisation and experience different aspects of its work.
2. Acting in different roles: You could offer opportunities for staff to act in roles that are one or two levels above their current position. This will give them a sense of the demands experienced in a higher role and help to develop their skills.
3. Support decision-making without taking over: Sometimes a staff member may need to make (or influence) a decision that is outside of their experience or beyond their current delegation. You can use this as an opportunity to develop their skills by working collaboratively to help them make the decision instead of stepping in and taking over. In these situations, lead from the side, not from the front.

A partnership approach

Effective leaders are workplace partners. They build teams that include a range of expertise and backgrounds. Great leaders recognise the value in diversity and encourage diverse thinking. They work alongside staff and make joint decisions about how to move the organisation forward. They ensure staff retain a sense of control over their work. They rarely tell people what to do or make decisions without consultation.

Good leaders remove obstacles and bring people together to make work happen. Effective leaders spend much of their time leading from the side.

Most of your success comes from your team

I estimate that around 80 per cent of leadership success is based in the effectiveness of the team. It comes from the entire team, not simply from the leader.

If I've got the 80 per cent right, then it means that just 20 per cent of team success is due to the strategic guidance and vision offered by you as the leader.

The smart people work with you

Sometimes leaders get stuck in a deficit mindset – they think that all the smart people work somewhere else, while their own team is sub-standard and in need of close management. This is not a productive perspective, and it's probably not true.

Don't discount the skills and experience in your current team. Instead, be thankful for what they offer and find ways to provide the support they need.

If your current team is not performing at the standard you seek, it's your job to do something about it. You can make change by providing opportunities for growth and development, and by hiring people with the best attitude.

Most importantly, you can make sure you're creating an environment where your staff can flourish. Don't constantly second guess their decisions. Don't make changes that are not needed. Instead, be clear about your vision, give your team clear limits about what they can and can't do, then get out of their way. Instead of being a manager, become a leader.

Get out of your people's way

There's a balance to good leadership. Yes, you need to lead people. But you also need to stand aside and let your people set their own path and reach their potential. You don't want to be the leader who stands in the way and makes things difficult for everyone.

Experienced leaders adjust their leadership style based on the current work environment and the experience of their team. A time of crisis might call for an escalation in hands-on leadership. An inexperienced team may require more direction. But the goal of a good leader in a business-as-usual environment should be a hands-off style that enables people to thrive.

People who are new to the team or inexperienced in their role are likely to need a lot of support and management. You'll need to teach them how to do things and give regular feedback about their performance. But as people gain experience, the management they need reduces. Good leaders can gradually step back and give more responsibility to their team.

Most senior leaders are involved in employment decisions about the most senior staff in the organisation, but they rarely participate in recruitment for lower-level positions. At the higher levels, employees are likely to be highly experienced, well-educated, competent people who need very little hands-on management. They don't need to be managed, but they do need good leadership.

With an experienced team, leadership involves setting an overall vision and direction, and providing mentoring when it's needed. What it doesn't involve is day-to-day management and checking that the work is being done correctly. If that's what you find yourself doing, you need to consider two possibilities. Firstly, is your leadership style the problem? Are you managing when you should be leading? Secondly, is your team lacking in experience? Do you need to provide opportunities for professional development to develop your team's ability to do the work?

It's a leader's job to help team members build their skills and experience. You need to provide support and remove roadblocks that stand in their way. Most importantly, you need to make sure you're not creating any roadblocks yourself. For example, when someone in the team encounters a challenge or problem, don't create a roadblock by stepping in and making things even more complex. At the same time, don't take over and dilute the opportunity for learning. Instead, work alongside the team member and solve the issue together. Provide leadership and support but let the team member do the work.

When you get out of your people's way, you're more likely to lead from the side than from the front. Instead of pulling people along behind you, you can become a partner – someone who supports and enables, and who lets people create their own path.

Remember that your team is critical to your success. Your job is to provide some level of inspiration and support, and then get out of your people's way.

Balance Compliance Versus Commitment

As a leader, how do you personally approach the balance between compliance and commitment? Do you generally demand compliance? Are you someone who seeks to gain commitment? Or do you strive for a balance between the two?

While all work demands at least some level of compliance, there's a strong argument to suggest that successful leaders are more likely to adopt a commitment mindset. They seek to encourage buy-in from people, rather than prioritising compliance.

Compliance suggests subservience

Compliance is defined as 'the act of conforming or yielding, a tendency to yield readily to others, especially in a weak or subservient way'.[20]

Some cultures value compliance, and these are typically cultures that prioritise tasks. They care about having the task completed and pay much less attention to whether people enjoy what they're doing. Worker satisfaction isn't an issue, because the outcome is more important than the team.

---
20. This definition comes from www.dictionary.com.

Businesses that focus on compliance tend to be process oriented. They worry about whether employees arrive on time and work the requisite number of minutes. They focus on whether each employee does all the required tasks, in the exact order required, using the exact methods required. They place little emphasis on employee development and overall strategic direction.

For many employees, working in a compliance-focused organisation is mindless. The leaders of compliance-focused organisations typically prioritise managing rather than leading – and within these organisations, good leadership is often lacking. They focus on box ticking ahead of strategy, with an excessive focus on policies and procedures. Task completion takes priority, ahead of everything else.

A potential outcome for compliance-focused organisations is that most staff don't understand how they fit into the overall organisation or how their work helps the organisation to achieve its mission. As a result, these organisations often experience little buy-in and commitment from their staff. Staff turnover may be high.

Commitment suggests organisational maturity

Commitment-focused organisations tend to have organisational maturity with a clear understanding of what they're doing and why. The focus shifts – away from box ticking and employee monitoring, towards longer-term goals and the best ways to achieve them.

Commitment can be defined as 'the state of being committed, the act of committing, pledging or engaging one's self, dedication, allegiance'.[21] The part of the definition that interests me most is the four key concepts at the end:

---

21. This definition comes from www.dictionary.com.

pledging, engaging oneself, dedication, and allegiance. For me, these concepts are the mark of a commitment-focused organisation.

When employees experience commitment, they want to be with you on the organisational journey. They believe in what the organisation is doing, and they want to be part of it. They believe in what the organisation is trying to achieve, and they feel accepted as an important part of the team. No matter what task they're responsible for, they understand how it fits into the organisation and contributes to what the entire team is doing. They understand that they are part of a team, working towards a common goal.

Commitment-focused organisations typically prioritise leadership ahead of management. The leaders work alongside people to build dedication and engagement. They don't need to demand compliance because it's willingly given.

A continuum, not opposed choices

No organisation is entirely commitment-focused or compliance-focused. What matters most is the balance between the two. The more you're able to shift towards a commitment-focused approach, the more likely you will be to build a strong, motivated, capable team.

The other thing about this continuum is that it's not static. There may be times of crisis, when compliance suddenly becomes critically important and, for a time, you need to shift more towards the compliance end of the continuum. And there may be other times – perhaps during the strategic planning cycle or while developing a particularly creative project – that you may be able to prioritise commitment even more than you normally do.

Reflect on your current commitment–compliance balance

Take a minute to reflect on commitment versus compliance from the perspective of your career.

How do you feel when you're on your way to work? Do you work in an environment where compliance matters more than commitment?

Is there a sense that everyone must turn up on time or that everything must be done a particular way? Is there a sense that the organisation is more process focused than outcomes focused?

Is there a sense that everyone's work is critically judged – perhaps even that identifying errors matters more than celebrating achievements?

Is there any possibility that the organisation's compliance focus makes people feel they don't want to be at work?

If the focus is weighted towards compliance, does your leadership style contribute? And is this something you'd like to change?

Aim to shift the balance

If you work in an organisation that prioritises compliance, you may like to think about whether you'd be happier working somewhere else. If you're not able to shift the balance from your position in the company, then changing jobs may be the right choice.

If your leadership style tends towards the compliance end of the spectrum, you may like to think about what steps you can take to shift the balance towards commitment. Make it your goal to ensure that you and your team feel positive about each workday because you all know your contribution matters.

Work should be a positive part of people's lives. It should be a source of satisfaction, interest, and engagement, not something that's all about sacrifice and anxiety. And it's possible that the balance between compliance and commitment is a key driver here.

As a leader, your task is to create an environment where your team will thrive. You're creating a workplace where people want to be doing things they value. This will make people feel empowered and give them a sense of control over their work. This empowerment will, in turn, encourage high levels of job satisfaction, and high levels of employee retention.

Communicate with Your Team

It probably won't come as any surprise to you to learn that most of my working life has involved being in organisations where communication sucks – particularly when it comes to providing feedback. It's an experience that you're likely to share with me. In fact, I don't think I've ever worked in a place where people comment about the terrific communication. Most of the time, communication within organisations isn't very good at all.

In this chapter, I want to share some of the things I've learned about communicating. I'm not suggesting that I'm a perfect communicator – I'm not even close to it! But I've given quite a lot of thought to the things that seem to matter most, and these are the things I try to improve in my own communication.

1. Be consistent: It's important to have a clear message and be consistent with that message. If you're trying to get a message across, then stay on message. Try to make sure the message remains consistent even when it's communicated in different ways. If you're asking multiple people to deliver a message on your behalf, consider providing notes to help improve consistency.

2. Use multiple methods: There are many different ways to communicate within an organisation, and important messages need to be communicated in as many ways as possible. Don't just rely on a single email. Combine your email with other methods – like announcements in meetings, signs or posters, social media or intranet sites, and maybe written documents. People may need to see your message multiple times before they pay attention.

3. Build in opportunities for feedback: Remember that communication is something that happens in multiple directions. You can't just send out a message and expect everyone to understand it and do what you ask. Make sure you provide opportunities for feedback and conversation.

4. Use a networking approach: In a large organisation, it's often not effective to try to communicate with everyone at the same time. And it's rarely effective for a large organisation to seek feedback using a centralised system. Instead, use your direct reports as communication intermediaries. Ask them to discuss the issue with their team, gather feedback, and then report back to you. Support this process at all levels of the organisation, so that everyone has an opportunity to contribute. Give people time to discuss the issue, develop their ideas, and report back.

5. Listen to what people say: When you build in opportunities for feedback, you need to be available and open. Genuinely listen to what people say.

6. Watch what people do: Sometimes people won't give you direct feedback, but you may be able to gather feedback from what people do and how they react.

Their actions (and inactions) may be an important source of feedback for you. Here's a simple example of this in practice. Sometimes when you're involved in a business that sells a product or service, the most useful feedback is how customers use what you're selling. Their buying habits and usage habits may give much greater insights than consumer feedback or endorsements. Whenever possible, set up systems that help you monitor people's actions, then use those insights to improve the way you work.

7. Remember that what you say may not be what people hear: It's easy to assume that everyone interprets messages the same way, but this isn't the case. Everyone interprets messages based on their individual understanding and context. You need to check in with people, seek feedback, and make sure their interpretation is what you meant them to understand.

An internal example of different interpretations

In one organisation, I was part of a major implementation project for a new system. We had special staff come in to manage the project with us. Early in the project, the project managers were on-site to meet with key people in the organisation. They discussed what the new system would do, what they hoped it would achieve, and how it would be used through the organisation. They spent around half a day working together on the project.

The next day, one of the key people involved in that meeting stopped by my office to ask when the consultation phase of the project would start and whether they would be involved. And the thing that struck me most was our differing perceptions of what had happened the previous day. To me and the project managers, that meeting had been the first step in the consultation process. But to key staff in the organisation, the half-day meeting had been an information session, not consultation. They'd felt talked to, not engaged in conversation.

Thankfully, that person's question put a spotlight on the problem, and we were able to address it quickly. Otherwise, the project could have got off to a rocky start.

An external example of different interpretations

I once worked in an organisation that employed several public facing staff. At one stage, the staff were having trouble with a member of the community who didn't understand the organisation and what we could do. The community member kept visiting our frontline staff and asking for help to solve an issue, but the issue was outside of our control and not related to the business we were involved in. Over time, the community member became threatening, and demanded that our frontline staff needed to help with the issue – which was, of course, impossible. For the frontline staff, the situation became increasingly difficult and stressful.

This was ultimately a communication challenge. We needed to find a way to help the community member understand that helping with this issue was beyond the scope of what the organisation could do.

Communicating what you don't do can be challenging – often much more challenging than communicating about what you can do. It's particularly difficult if the work you do seems in some way relevant but isn't quite the same.

Developing a shared language

One way to support clear communication is to develop a shared language with your audiences. This can be challenging – particularly in our multicultural communities. We have multiple languages, different customs, and different approaches to non-verbal communication. People also have different communication expectations based on their education and experience – which may be linked to different roles within the organisation. Any of these things can create communication barriers.

Developing a shared language and providing opportunities for clear communication takes time. We need to pause and check whether people understand what we're trying to communicate. We need to check that we're not unintentionally confusing people or causing cultural offence.

It's a particular leadership responsibility to invest the time required for clear communication. You don't just want to be understood; you also want to understand. And that means you need to create an environment where people can let you know if your communication is causing a problem. Take the time to check people's understanding and check you're communicating in a way that's appropriate.

Don't discount the jargon of your industry

Industry jargon is a shared language – a type of verbal shorthand that helps you to communicate clearly and precisely. When everyone understands the jargon, it's a highly effective part of your communication.

But it's important to remember that new staff, customers, and people working in other industries may not understand your jargon. Sometimes, your abbreviations and terms will mean something completely different to people in another organisation.

It's helpful to reflect on when and how you use the jargon of your industry or your workplace. Use it when it's helpful and avoid it when it's not.

To challenge yourself, try to describe what you do using only plain language that someone without a technical background could understand. This will help to wake you up to the jargon you use every day, often without giving it a second thought. I often do this when I'm in a group of fellow veterans. We all try to describe our jobs in the military to someone who has never had any military involvement. It's a challenge, and it helps us to realise just how specialised our shared jargon can be.

Always prioritise communication

As a leader, you need to prioritise communication with your team. Focus on communicating frequently and clearly, and make sure you leave the door open for feedback. Communicating with people is not the same as sending emails or relying on social media. You need to engage with people in a personal way – either by phone or face-to-face.

I often respond to an email with a quick phone call. It's often the most efficient way to address the issue. And it shows people that I care enough to want to discuss the issue directly with them. People who are new to working with me tend to find it a bit odd at first. But they soon appreciate it for what it is: a genuine attempt to communicate clearly, listen, and respond to feedback.

Focus on Your People

If your goal is to be the best leader you can be, you need to put time, effort, and resources into the people you lead. Focus on your people, and the rest is likely to follow.

Provide opportunities for staff development

Effective leaders provide opportunities for their staff to seek professional development and learn new skills. They know that motivated staff need to feel they're making some progress in their careers, and they provide opportunities for this to happen.

Professional development doesn't have to involve costly conferences or workshops. There are many other, less costly ways to help staff to develop. Maybe you can share books about leadership or other books relevant to the workplace. Maybe you can organise a book club or reading group. Maybe you can organise lunchtime discussions about professional development issues. Maybe your workplace would benefit from an internal mentoring program. Maybe you can ask people in the workplace to run short seminars about their area of expertise. None of these ideas is costly.

Sometimes, a useful approach to professional development involves allocating time for teams to learn from each other. Maybe your human resources staff could spend time shadowing the finance team. Or maybe the finance team could shadow the marketing team. Simple approaches to sharing information across the organisation will give your team a much broader understanding of the work that's being done.

In large organisations, it's often possible to move people between teams every few years – in a way that helps people to build their skills and develop new interests. Smaller organisations may not have the ability to do this. But even in small organisations, you can implement small mentoring or shadowing schemes that give people an idea of work across the organisation.

Challenge staff with increased delegation

One way to help staff to develop new skills is to offer increased opportunities for delegation.

Perhaps you could start with your own role. What tasks can you reasonably delegate to someone else? Make sure you choose tasks that will be meaningful for the person who takes them on.

If you choose to delegate tasks to create new challenges for other staff, remember that you're delegating the authority to do the task but not the responsibility to ensure it's done correctly. Even when you delegate, you still hold responsibility for ensuring the task is completed on time and with competence. But even though you retain final responsibility, delegation can still be worthwhile for everyone involved.

Listen to what your people need

One of the best ways to develop as a leader is to listen closely to your people and provide them with support. Encourage them to verbalise their questions or objections. Invite them to comment on the way work is done. Listen to their input – whether it's positive or negative. Respond by engaging with them and truly trying to understand their perspective. Don't shut them down with a quick reaction about why something is done in a particular way.

When your people bring ideas and suggestions to you, it's important to engage with those ideas, show that you respect the person for speaking up, and back up the new idea. This doesn't mean that you need to agree with every suggestion. But it does mean you need to take it seriously.

When you give a team member the go-ahead to try something new, make sure you're prepared to back them all the way. If something goes wrong, don't turn your back on the new idea or say you always knew it wouldn't work. Instead, back up the person, follow through with your approval, and do what you can to sort out the problem. Draw on your experience to help figure things out.

Remember to accept failure

If you're trying out new ideas, you're almost certain to experience failure every so often. Not every idea can be successful – particularly not the first time it's tried.

When we fail at something, we learn. We learn much more from failures than we do from successes. So, if a member of your team tries out a new idea and it fails, see it as a great learning opportunity. It's unlikely that the failure is on a scale that will be catastrophic enough to destroy the company. While the failure may bring some pain, it's a great opportunity to learn. It's also an opportunity for you to show that you thoroughly support your team and applaud their efforts to try something new.

If you're working with a great team, it's likely that the team will work together to minimise the impact of any failure. The failure may simply become a roadblock that you need to navigate around. By focusing on your people, you can help to build the strength and motivation required to pick up and keep moving when things get tough.

You're standing in their way

In all organisations, leaders stand in the way of staff who are lower on the hierarchy. This isn't a negative thing – it's a simple reality. If you have motivated staff who want to be promoted through the organisation, then their supervisors and managers stand in their way. If you're in a senior leadership position, you'll be standing in the way of a lot of people.

One implication of this is that you shouldn't feel disappointed or cheated when staff move to a different organisation to advance their career. If you've provided them with sufficient opportunities for growth, at some stage they're going to want more challenge or more opportunity. And while a large organisation can often locate those opportunities, smaller organisations cannot. And that means they need to leave your team to continue growing.

Good leaders recognise this as a realistic outcome of hard work, and support staff when it happens. They don't try to hold onto a staff member who is valuable in that position if it's clear that further growth isn't possible in the organisation. They certainly don't put pressure on the staff member to stay in their current role because that's the easiest option for the organisation. Instead, they support the staff member to leave on good terms, recognising the movement as the inevitable consequence of a strong team.

Supporting your staff to leave on good terms makes good business sense. It's a way of building your network and extending that network out into other organisations. When your other staff see this in action, they're more likely to put more time and effort into their own career development.

If you find that head-hunters are seeking out your staff and trying to recruit people away from your organisation, take it as a compliment. Yes, it's frustrating. But it's also an indication that the good people work for you, and you've done a great job in developing them. You never know, this person might be the one who comes back and replaces you one day.

Let Others Hold You Accountable

As a leader, you'll create a more open, trusting environment if you make it clear that you're giving other people permission to hold you accountable. It's a way of demonstrating that everyone needs someone to help them stay focused on the best way forward. I suggest that you find yourself an accountability partner.

There are two different ways to ensure you're held to account, and which one you choose will depend on what makes you feel most comfortable. You could choose a close friend or close colleague to be your accountability partner – someone you know and trust – and explicitly give them permission to hold you accountable. Alternatively, you could choose a professional colleague – someone you're less comfortable with but you trust – and set up an explicit agreement about accountability. For some people, choosing a professional colleague makes more sense, because there are fewer relationship issues involved and accountability discussions seem more comfortable. It's possible that you could become accountability partners for each other.

The common thread here is that you need to explicitly invite someone to be your accountability partner. Accountability becomes an agreed part of your relationship with that person.

Welcome the challenge

When your accountability partner questions you about something, remember that they're doing exactly what you asked them to do. You may feel challenged or disappointed with yourself, but it's important that you don't let yourself be upset. Instead, be thankful the person cares enough to bring it up. Try to accept the accountability questions in the spirit of improvement – reflect on whatever it is, question your own behaviours and motivations, and engage in a conversation about what's going on.

Remember that your accountability partner is there to help you stay on track. They're trying to help you, and they've got your best interests at heart. While you may feel challenged by whatever it is they've noticed, it's important to accept what they're saying and reflect with an open mind. Make sure that you don't get angry with the messenger.

Link your accountability to your key performance indicators

In workplaces, we have key performance indicators (KPIs) that hold us accountable. I like to use the same approach right across my personal and professional life. I develop KPIs – which are, of course, nothing more than simple goals – and ask my accountability partner to help me focus on achieving them.

It's a good idea to share your personal and professional goals with an accountability partner. I know it's tempting to keep these things private – perhaps because you don't want people to know your goals just in case you fail. But sharing your goals and discussing them with someone will help you to stay focused. If your accountability partner understands your goals, then they'll help you out if you fall behind. If you have an accountability partner who has your best interests at heart, they'll hold you to account in a highly positive way. They'll want you to achieve whatever goals you've set for yourself, and their support makes it more likely that you'll succeed.

Let your accountability partner challenge your progress

A good accountability partner will ask you questions about whether you're achieving your goals and will help you to stay focused. You may find that your accountability partner becomes an important sounding board for you – someone you can talk to about the things you're struggling with or the roadblocks that are making it difficult to achieve your goals. Some accountability partners are able to offer direct advice, based on their own experiences doing similar things. Others will work with you to solve the problem together.

Having an accountability partner will help you to achieve challenging goals more quickly. They'll help you to maintain your focus and prevent you from slipping backwards.

I believe that one of the main reasons people fail to achieve their goals is that they don't have anyone to hold them accountable. If you don't share your goals and you've got no one who is challenging you to keep moving forward, your goals will be much more difficult to achieve. Having an accountability partner is a way to avoid that problem.

Managing Up – and Why You Should Do It

Managing up is something that tends to come up in conversation when someone is struggling with their supervisor. The conversation typically focuses on how to manage up – that is, what the person can do to influence the behaviour of their supervisor.

But I believe managing up shouldn't be kept aside as a strategy for dealing with incompetent supervisors. It's something you should be doing all the time.

My logic is simple: you were employed to be as effective as possible. And one of the ways to achieve that is to ensure your supervisor is as effective and successful as possible. It's something you can achieve, at least in part, by managing up.

Managing up can mean a whole variety of things. It might mean supporting your supervisor to develop their skills, removing barriers that are in their way, helping them create an efficient working environment, or helping to create high levels of workplace satisfaction. Whatever it involves, ultimately what you're doing is influencing the work of your supervisor.

Don't be the supervisor staff want to replace

According to an article I read recently, around 65 per cent of people would prefer to have a new boss over a pay rise.[22] Think about that for a moment. It means that most workers are so unhappy with their supervisor that they'd prefer a new supervisor ahead of more money.

You don't want to be the supervisor or leader that staff would prefer to replace. That's not a path that can work out well for you, your team, or your organisation. If you've got high staff turnover, remember that people typically leave people, not organisations. You need to make it your business to ensure people want to work with you.

Most people want to work for supervisors who are competent, trustworthy, and motivating. They want to be stimulated and interested by work.

Eight strategies for managing up

A 2015 article in *Harvard Business Review* provides useful insights on this topic.[23] It describes eight situations when employees should strive to manage up.

1. Manage up to help a new supervisor grow into their role

All new supervisors – whether they're recently promoted from within the organisation or brought in from outside – will

---

22. Discussed in '65% of Americans Choose a Better Boss Over a Raise – Here's Why' by Ty Kiisel, 16 October 2012, *Forbes* (https://www.forbes.com/sites/tykiisel/2012/10/16/65-of-americans-choose-a-better-boss-over-a-raise-heres-why/?sh=7057589076d2).
23. 'What Everyone Should Know About Managing Up' by Dana Rousmaniere, 23 January 2015, *Harvard Business Review* (https://hbr.org/2015/01/what-everyone-should-know-about-managing-up).

need time to grow into their role. Every new supervisor needs to learn how the team works, what their role involves, and what's expected of them. Their team members can help with this, by providing information and support. Managing up in this situation will help the new supervisor to settle quickly into their role.

2. Support managers you rarely see face-to-face

In some organisations, staff rarely see their supervisors face-to-face. This is becoming increasingly common, with geographically dispersed organisations and staff working from home. Having little face-to-face contact with staff can create challenges for managers. It's more difficult for them to understand their team's work styles and support needs. It's also more difficult to communicate regularly. In these circumstances, staff can manage up by ensuring they communicate clearly and frequently with their managers, and by providing sufficient information for managers to understand their work styles.

3. Manage up when your supervisor lacks confidence or feels insecure

Sometimes your manager may appear to be insecure – perhaps because they're new in their role, perhaps because they're not confident about their skills, or perhaps because they feel threatened by you. If this happens, try to understand why your manager is lacking confidence and put in place some strategies that will help you to respond in the best way possible.

4. Manage up if your supervisor is indecisive

Some managers don't seem capable of making a decision, and this can be hugely frustrating for their staff. In this circumstance, managing up can involve working closely with the person and supporting them to make decisions. Then, once a decision has been made, you can work to implement it quickly to ensure it's well under way before they change their mind.

5. Manage up if you receive conflicting messages

If you work for someone who gives conflicting messages, you never quite know what you're going to encounter when you arrive at work. If the team's vision or tasks are constantly changing, it's enormously frustrating for staff. It creates a work environment with very little satisfaction for employees. Manage up by reminding this manager about their previous decisions and encouraging them to be consistent.

6. Manage up if you have a long-winded boss

Some people just love to talk. They take forever to get to the point, and it can be very difficult to hold your tongue. If your manager has this problem, it's not often practical to say, 'will you please just get to the point?'. It's difficult to manage up in this circumstance without seeming disrespectful. But you can try summarising what you've heard so far, asking highly focused questions, and always ensuring that your own communication is succinct.

7. Manage up if you have a hands-off boss

Some managers prefer to give their staff a lot of freedom and adopt a highly hands-off approach to supervision. This particularly happens with experienced managers and high-performing staff, when there's a lot of trust in the team and little need for constant oversight. It can also happen if a manager knows someone is not performing well but doesn't know how to address the issue.

Managers need to be careful not to give staff so much freedom that the staff end up feeling unsupported. The sweet spot is a happy medium, where staff have an appropriate level of support based on their skills, confidence, and experience.

If you're stuck in a situation where your manager adopts an excessively hands-off approach, the best thing you can do is talk to the manager about it. Explain that you need the manager's engagement and support. Let them know what you feel and what you need. Explain that you'll be able to work more effectively if you're given more support.

8. Manage up if your boss isn't as smart as you

Sometimes you'll be more experienced, more quick thinking, or simply cleverer than the person who is managing you. It's actually quite a sound strategy as a manager to employ people who are smarter than you are yourself. I try to do it all the time, because I want to work with the smartest, most experienced team possible. I want to employ someone who fills a gap in the organisation – and preferably someone who fills a gap in my own skills.

If your manager can see that you're good at your job, they should celebrate this. When you perform well, your manager looks good. You can manage up in these circumstances by showing your manager what you can do well and making it clear that you're contributing in a way that brings benefit to the whole team.

How to manage up when your supervisor lacks competence

Another useful article on this topic was published in *Forbes* in May 2018 by Rodger Dean Duncan.[24] In the article, Duncan

---

24. 'Why Managing Up Is a Skill Set You Need' by Rodger Dean Duncan, 26 May 2018, *Forbes* (https://www.forbes.com/sites/rodgerdeanduncan/2018/05/26/why-managing-up-is-a-skillset-you-need/).

interviews Mary Abbajay, author of a book about managing up.[25] In her conversation with Duncan, Abbajay discusses several strategies for managing up when your immediate manager lacks competence. I've summarised a few of her strategies here.

De-escalate your anger

Firstly, Abbajay suggests that you'll benefit if you can de-escalate your anger. It's natural to feel angry if your manager lacks competence, but your anger won't help. Feeling angry will undermine your thoughts and direct your actions. It will prevent you from making careful decisions and may make the situation worse. Abbajay suggests that people in this situation should try to put themselves into their manager's shoes. Imagine what it would be like to suspect that you lacked the competence required for the job. If this was you, how would you want to be treated by your staff? Instead of anger, can you treat the manager with respect?

Abbajay goes beyond respect and suggests that it makes sense to replace anger with something like empathy or compassion. If you start with the understanding that your manager isn't yet competent for the role – but will be with more experience – you'll be able to support them in their learning and help them to increase their competence.

Diagnose the incompetence

Abbajay suggests that it's helpful to specifically diagnose the incompetence. For example, maybe your boss is new to the role and hasn't developed all the skills required, or perhaps they haven't developed a sufficient level of emotional intelligence.

---

25. *Managing Up: How to Move up, Win at Work, and Succeed with Any Type of Boss* by Mary Abbajay, 2018, John Wiley & Sons.

You can work with your boss and try to enable their development. If that fails, in these situations it often makes sense to approach it with a sense of humour. Instead of getting angry, find the funny side. Learn from it, then move on.

However, I strongly urge you not to act against your boss, given their position in the organisation. I've seen team members who try to expose their boss's incompetence or undermine their boss within the organisation. This seldom works out in the team member's best interests. Often, it simply highlights that the team member has a low level of emotional intelligence and poor upward management – suggesting they're not ready for any type of leadership position.

Another unsuccessful strategy I've seen is where a team member refuses to do certain tasks for their incompetent manager. If you do this, it's likely that you'll be marginalised and potentially viewed as less competent yourself.

Compensate and cover

According to Abbajay, another useful approach is to compensate and cover – which can be a useful strategy for both managers and staff.

When a manager recognises they're not yet fully competent in their role or there's an area of work where they'll never be particularly strong, they can bring people into the team who will help to fill the gaps. Managers who can self-diagnose this type of problem and build a team that compensates for their weaknesses will have the greatest likelihood of success. In these circumstances, it makes sense to be completely open with the team about what is happening. If you're a manager, let people know that you recognise the areas where you need the most support.

Sometimes a team member will recognise a manager's weakness and will compensate and cover for the manager.

If the manager is a strong leader, they will be aware of their weaknesses and, most importantly, will recognise that you're compensating or covering for them. When this happens, it can go a long way to increasing the levels of trust and success in the team.

The idea that team members and managers can compensate and cover links well with the idea that a successful leader will build a team with complementary skills. Their goal is to build a team of people who can work together and compensate for each other's weaknesses. You don't want a team where everyone has the same skills and abilities. Instead, you want diversity among the team, with a balance of skills to ensure you're best able to address complex challenges.

Look for technical competence

Abbajay suggests that bosses who lack managerial competence may be competent in a more technical way. After all, at some point in this manager's career, someone chose to promote them ahead of everyone else. Someone in the organisation felt this person was suitable for the job. Try to figure out why that is. Look for hidden strengths – particularly technical strengths – that explain how the manager got this position. Chances are that they were highly skilled and competent – and maybe they still are. Abbajay suggests that it may be worth taking the time to learn from this person's technical expertise. This could be a great opportunity to hone your own skills.

If managing up is difficult and you feel that your manager clearly lacks competence, maybe you can use it as an opportunity to learn more about what poor management looks like. Reflect on what's happening and think about how you might work differently.

Your Industry Isn't Special

I have a background working across different industries – including defence, accounting, manufacturing, environment, corporate, hospital and health services, tertiary education, research, and mining. Each of these industries has its own dynamics.

People often ask me how I'm able to work across so many different industries. But it's not actually so difficult. All organisations have things in common. They all have people, processes, and governance principles. Yes, I need to develop industry knowledge to work effectively, but that can usually be gained quite quickly. Given that I don't work in highly technical roles, I'm able to start with my understanding of strategic principles and team dynamics and quickly build the industry understanding I need.

Something similar applies at the board level. A well-functioning board includes members with a wide range of skills and experience – they're not all experts in the technical field of this particular organisation. The business owner or CEO needs strong industry knowledge – particularly about the legislative requirements facing the industry. They may also need technical expertise. But board members and other senior leaders bring different types of knowledge and contribute to different aspects of the business.

Lack of industry experience can be a benefit

In some cases, it's my lack of industry experience that brings most value to the organisation I'm working with. Because I bring a broad, outsider's perspective, I can sometimes identify inefficiencies or opportunities that technical experts can't see. I'm able to bring my experience from a wide range of industries and apply it to the particular issues I recognise in the organisation. In this way, I can often bring new approaches that help to increase the organisation's revenue, develop efficiencies, or improve employee satisfaction.

Some CEOs and boards will question whether a person without industry experience can truly understand their operations and improve things. They may be committed to the ways they currently do things and may be reluctant to change. You can only take your outsider perspective so far. While you may be able to see opportunities for change and improvement, you won't be able to achieve much if the organisation is committed to the status quo. Instead, you may be seen as an unwelcome challenger. In these circumstances, you may need to tread carefully and establish your credibility before proposing change.

Being resistant to change

Most people don't like change. They like the way they do things, and they don't want to do the hard work of introducing something new. In addition, many people in organisations are conflict averse and don't like having difficult conversations.

As a leader, if you're willing to engage in difficult conversations and you're good at bringing about change, you'll probably be successful in just about any industry you choose to work in. But you may experience roadblocks from industry leaders with extensive knowledge and experience who want to retain the status quo.

I believe that all organisations need to evolve and adapt. They need to embrace new technologies and find new ways of working. They need to understand how their customers and clients are changing. They need to respond to new preferences and demands.

Disruptive change from technology

All industries are facing disruptive change from new technology. The businesses that thrive will be the ones that embrace new technologies and adapt the ways they work.

A good example here is the mining industry. In the past, mining relied on a huge workforce for tasks such as excavating and hauling. Increasingly, this work is automated, with fewer staff required. Automation and AI are replacing people. These organisations need to find new ways of working, and their staff need to find new employment.

Tertiary education is another industry that's facing massive upheaval. Lecture theatres are no longer filled with students. Instead, many students now study online and rarely visit their campus. Many students juggle study with work, and don't have the luxury of committing to fixed-time classes.

These disruptions bring difficulties and opportunities – and it's the leader's job to understand them and respond to them. Into the future, I believe we'll see more and more people who work across multiple industries. Strategic thinking skills are portable and industry agnostic.

Hire for behaviours not skills

This brings me to an important point about employing new staff. When you're hiring people into senior positions, it makes sense to hire for their behaviours, not for their technical ability. Look for people who can think strategically, build strong teams, communicate clearly, and achieve results. Be less worried about their years of experience in your industry.

6 Principles for KPIs

Lots of people talk about key performance indicators (KPIs) and most people agree they're valuable. Developing great KPIs is both art and science – and maybe it's more of an art than most people realise.

Developing great KPIs is difficult, and people who do it well are not easy to find. But when they're done right, KPIs are a powerful catalyst of organisational success. With good KPIs, you'll be amazed at what you can achieve.

Ideally, you should have KPIs for every role, at every level of the organisation. But in practice, this is rare. Many organisations develop team-wide or even organisation-wide KPIs. This approach dilutes their value.

In this chapter, I share six principles for developing strong KPIs that are linked to role descriptions right across the organisation.

1. Ensure each KPI is relevant to the organisation's strategy

KPIs can't be developed until you have figured out your strategic direction and, ideally, developed your strategic plan. You don't need a long, detailed strategic plan – a one page summary of your overall strategic direction is sufficient, if that's all you have. Without an understanding of the organisation's strategic direction, you can't ensure the KPIs you develop will contribute towards achieving it. And that's their main purpose: KPIs break down targets to help everyone in the organisation contribute to the strategic direction.

2. Ensure each KPI is relevant to the role

Each role description needs specific KPIs that are relevant to the work done by the people filling those roles.

Too often, organisations work from their strategic plan to develop organisational KPIs, perhaps alongside something like a balanced scorecard. These organisational KPIs show how the strategic direction will be achieved, but they rarely filter down well to roles across the organisation.

For example, a financial goal may be to increase the organisation's gross profit by 50 per cent over two years. That might be a reasonable KPI for the finance team, but how does an individual staff member contribute to that? What is its specific impact on their workload or sales targets?

Translating the strategic KPI to a role-level KPI will help people to understand how they fit into the organisation's strategic path. The result is a meaningful KPI that staff can reasonably work towards.

3. Ensure KPIs are within the individual's control

KPIs need to be relevant to the work an individual is doing. They also need to be realistic and achievable. If they're not, the KPIs are simply setting people up for failure.

Too often, organisations develop high-level KPIs, then expect them to trickle down through the organisation without specifically applying them to the work done at each level. What happens is that individual staff look at their KPIs and conclude that the KPIs they're being asked to work towards are not relevant to their work, not achievable, or not practical.

They may also conclude that they're going to be measured against something they are unable to influence. When staff members are asked to work towards KPIs that are outside of their control, they're likely to become frustrated and stressed.

The best approach here is to consult with staff about relevant KPIs. If you involve staff in setting their KPIs, you're providing them with a sense of control and jointly developing something they can feel committed to.

4. KPIs need to be limited in number

It's not realistic to ask staff to work towards a seemingly endless list of KPIs. It's also not relevant to make every task a KPI.

KPIs should be reasonably large, important activities that move the organisation towards its goals. KPIs should not be linked to standard parts of a job – like working the requisite number of hours or submitting an agreed number of reports.

You don't need to turn everything you measure into a KPI. In fact, the more KPIs you have, the more you reduce the likelihood of them being achieved. It's not possible to perform well on a wide variety of targets. Instead, you need to focus.

As a general principle, keep the number of KPIs small (maybe between three and five) and ensure they function as high-level indicators of the organisation's progress.

5. Review KPIs regularly

KPIs are important, and it doesn't make sense to review them just once a year. Instead, review KPIs either quarterly or monthly. This gives you a regular opportunity to check on progress and adjust the KPIs if necessary.

Make sure you don't develop KPIs and never refer to them again. Supervisors should ensure they regularly make time to discuss KPIs with their staff. Regular opportunities to check in will make it more likely that staff will achieve their KPIs.

Regular review of KPIs will help you to quickly identify where the organisation is doing well. It will also help you to identify gaps and bottlenecks, perhaps providing an opportunity to take action before problems escalate.

If you notice that staff are not achieving their KPIs, you may need to discuss their performance and consider additional training. But most of the time, you're likely to discover that it's the KPIs that need to change, not the person. A quarterly review helps you to identify KPIs that are either unrealistic or inappropriate, giving you an opportunity to make change immediately instead of waiting until the next planning cycle.

6. Ensure KPIs are achievable

It makes sense to view KPIs as targets you genuinely want staff to achieve. KPIs should be realistic and clearly achievable. They're not so-called 'stretch targets' that some people might reach if they're lucky.

I once worked in an organisation that adopted industry standard KPIs. The KPIs were in no way unusual, yet only around 5 per cent of the staff ever achieved them. My task was to help figure out what was causing the problem. The problem wasn't an unskilled workforce or a poor organisational culture. Instead, the poor KPI achievement was caused by inefficient internal processes and systems.

This organisation was never going to achieve the industry standard KPIs because the background systems being used were making this impossible. In response, we embarked on a major update of the organisation's process. And the next time we measured our KPI outcomes, we suddenly had 95 per cent of the workforce achieving their KPIs! We achieved huge cost savings for the organisation, plus significant improvements in both employee and client satisfaction. Suddenly the organisation's staff developed a sense of pride and accomplishment in their work. A natural by-product of this was that client numbers grew, and revenue improved.

This result had nothing to do with the KPIs – which did not change. It simply involved understanding why the KPIs were not achievable and removing the source of the problem.

There's another side to this point about having achievable KPIs. If you have a high-performing employee who achieves their goals, it's important that you don't expand their KPIs and try to squeeze more out of them. While this may be successful in the short term, in the longer term it presents multiple risks – including employee burnout or reduced employee satisfaction. Make sure that escalating KPIs don't encourage your employees to leave.

The Goldilocks KPI

Developing strong KPIs is all about balance. You need them to be challenging, but just challenging enough. The Goldilocks principle applies here – you're after just the right balance. When you get the balance right for each employee, you'll improve the likelihood that you're leading a very high-achieving organisation.

The Value of Money

How do we value money? It's an arbitrary concept. The value of something is nothing more than what you're willing to pay for it or trade it for.

I used to do an exercise in workshops, where I put $5 down on the table and asked what participants thought it was worth. Silly question, right? It's worth $5 of course. True – but what's the value of that $5? People get there eventually. The $5 is just a piece of paper or polymer, with little true value. It's only worth $5 because that's what written on it and that's what we've agreed it's worth as a community.

If a central bank decides that a piece of paper or polymer is worth $5, then people will accept its value. But it's possible to put any value on that polymer or paper. The $5 is no different from the $50, except for its colour, illustration, and the number printed on it. As a community, we agree that the $50 is worth 10 of the $5.

Currencies have a geographical reach, which limits where they can be used and how they're valued. Bank notes and coins usually have no value outside their country of origin. While the notes can be exchanged in a bank, the coins become worthless. Even in a digital form, working between currencies involves transfers and additional costs.

Something similar applies with products and services. Their value is what a purchaser is willing to pay, and their value may not translate between countries.

Sometimes it's an emotional connection that creates value – and this means that what's valuable to one person may not be of value to someone else. If you're able to break the emotional connection with money and think more objectively about true value, you may find that you change your decisions about the value of certain things.

When I worked in accounting, I would tell the accountants that many people – including business owners and executives – don't care about the numbers. They care about the business. They're more interested in the overall state of the business than in the actual numbers. A set of financial statements is a reflection of what has happened in the business, and the numbers in the balance sheet or profit and loss statement are a by-product of something that has happened. The numbers reflect things that have happened, including sales, production, and business decisions. Numbers aren't based on emotions, but the state of the business frequently is. It makes sense to be unemotional about the numbers and emotional about what's happening in the business.

Most Decisions Are Made with Emotion

Most people make decisions based on emotion. Emotion typically takes precedence, ahead of logical reasoning. People think about what they want, how they feel about the decision, what benefits they'll gain from the decision, and what they might lose if they don't make this decision. Even though many people believe they make their decisions through analytical reasoning, for most of us this isn't true. Analytical reasoning plays just a small role – a long way behind emotion.

Buying a house is a good example here. It's the biggest purchase most people make. The buyer's goal is to choose the house that's the best fit for them and their family. But instead of analysing property data and conducting a hard analysis of the benefits and drawbacks of each property, most buyers choose based on whether they feel the house is a good fit for them. They try to imagine themselves living in the house and use that to make a decision.

Even in business, it appears that most decisions – even the major ones – are heavily swayed by emotion. In business we present all kinds of analytical, quantitative data, often supported by detailed qualitative research. All too often, the people making decisions don't take the time to carefully interrogate the analytical information. Instead, they make their decisions based on their feelings or gut instinct.

If you find yourself in a situation that is emotionally charged, take a pause and try to separate yourself from the situation. You may like to ask someone who is not directly involved to review the situation and give you advice – perhaps someone from your trusted network.

One strategy I try to invoke when making decisions is to question myself about whether I have any personal interests linked to this decision and whether they could be affecting my judgement. If I'm conscious of personal interests, I invite someone else to review the information with me. I deliberately seek out someone with a different perspective from my own. I've found that this approach helps to broaden my thinking and encourage me to consider different perspectives. It has definitely improved my decision-making.

TED Talks and Other Difficult Conversations

We've all got things we'd prefer to avoid – things that make us nervous or things we know we're not particularly good at. For me, one of those things is public speaking. I find public speaking challenging, and I'd really prefer to avoid it.

In mid-2015, I was working for a company that sponsored a local TEDx. Because I worked for the sponsor, I wasn't allowed to speak at the event. But at some time during the planning, I mentioned that I'd like to do a TEDx Talk one day. I thought it would be a great challenge for me and something I'd enjoy.

Flash forward to 2017, and I received an email saying I had been nominated to deliver a TEDx Talk. To say that I was surprised is an understatement. It turned out that someone had overheard my comment in 2015 and had put my name forward.

For some reason, I thought that preparing my TEDx Talk would be straightforward. I expected the presentation itself to be a challenge, but I was confident about my approach to preparation. I had my four-step process figured out: identify the topic, write the talk, rehearse until I was flawless, then deliver a great talk that would go viral. Maybe I was caught up in a self-developed myth!

What actually happened was that I sat down to start step one, which should have been simple, and hit decision paralysis. I had no idea what to talk about! The whole premise of TED Talks is that people discuss ideas worth spreading. And I suddenly felt that I had absolutely no ideas valuable enough for that category. I felt like an imposter, with no expertise in any subject.

My decision paralysis and imposter syndrome led to procrastination – which of course is exactly the wrong approach to this sort of work. Procrastinating simply exacerbates the problem! My hope was that I'd have a last-minute stroke of genius which would leave me with enough time to cram in my preparation. But in my dreams, I imagined having a nervous breakdown on stage, which quickly went viral and meant that I could never show my face in public again.

One evening when I was busy alternating worry with procrastination, my five-year-old son came over to ask me what I was doing. I said that I was trying to write a TED Talk and explained a bit about how TED Talks work. He nodded his head as though he understood, and said it sounded like fun.

And his comment got me thinking. He said the talk sounded like fun! And back in 2015, I'd thought it would be fun. But I wasn't having fun at all. I was so caught up in anxiety that I couldn't even settle on a topic. My son's comment repositioned my thinking and encouraged me to have more fun. And suddenly I had my topic.

I decided that my topic would be: *Stop acting like an adult and start thinking like a five-year-old.*

And with that topic in hand, I went through my four-step process. I controlled my nerves, delivered a talk that was well received, and lived to see another day. Of course, I didn't go viral and become an overnight sensation, but I probably always knew that wasn't going to happen.

Since doing that TEDx Talk, I've talked about the experience at a number of team building workshops. After I've taken people through the process, I show them the YouTube video of my talk. And then I ask some simple questions. Did they laugh as they were watching? No, that didn't happen. Did anyone there at my TEDx Talk laugh at me until I was forced to leave the stage? No, that didn't happen. Did anyone throw things at me or try to hurt me? No, that didn't happen. Did I perform so badly that I damaged my reputation? No, that didn't happen either.

Leading up to the event, I believed that people would laugh at me or hate what I planned to say. But that rarely happens. And that got me thinking about some useful lessons for people who, like me, would prefer to avoid difficult presentations.

You are the main limit of your success

When it comes to public speaking, you as the speaker are typically the main limit of your success. If you believe you'll fail, you make things much more difficult for yourself. Most of the time, the positives of public speaking far outweigh the negatives.

My TEDx Talk wasn't hugely original, but my perspective was. The stories I told hadn't been told before. People welcomed my perspective and listened to it.

Having done something like a TEDx Talk is hugely beneficial. It's something that many people look favourably on. It's an achievement to be proud of, and it looks good in the CV.

Several people came up to me after my talk and said that they'd love to do something like that themselves – but they couldn't because they could never get up and speak like that in front of strangers. If you believe you can't do it, then you never will. But if you reframe your thinking, you'll discover that you – like most people – are perfectly capable of getting up there and speaking to a group. Yes, it's hard, but you can do it. No one is going to hurt you, and it's not going to be a disaster.

Think outside your old limits

The theme of my talk applies here. If you want to achieve something new, then stop thinking like an adult and start to challenge your old parameters and limits. Age may bring wisdom and knowledge, but often it also brings limits. As we age, we tend to become more set in our ways and more convinced that the parameters we've set for ourselves are real. We believe we're capable of some things and not capable of others.

It's possible that you tell yourself you can't do something because you had particular fears drilled into you as a child. Maybe you believe that what you've always done is the only thing you're capable of. Maybe you believe the things your parents said about you are true. To challenge this, imagine that you're a child who doesn't understand the boundaries imposed by the world. To a five-year-old, nothing is impossible. When you're five, you believe you can do anything if you put your mind to it.

Here's an example about how my son challenged the limits of my thinking. It's a story I shared in the TEDx Talk. One night, my son washed his hair using a new shampoo. Both his mother and I talked about how good it smelled, and my son wanted to smell it himself. As an adult, I told him this was impossible – he couldn't get his nose to reach his hair. And being five, he thought of a solution. He asked if it would work if he used a straw. So, we tried it – with one end of the straw in his hair, and the other end to his nose. It worked! It's a neat example of how a child can find solutions to all sorts of things.

Different background, similar goals

Another thing I learned from my son and articulated in the TEDx Talk is that children are accepting of other people in a way that adults may not be. Children are rarely interested in race, religion, or political beliefs. On a playground, for example, children just want to have a good time. They accept other children from all sorts of backgrounds and perspectives, and happily play together. Other children can arrive halfway through a game, and still be accepted.

This isn't so easy in the workplace. As adults, we often put too much emphasis on our differences, and fail to focus on our shared goals. It's shared goals that create successful teams.

Make sure it's fun

The most important thing I learned from my TEDx Talk is that work should be fun. Yes, there's hard work too, but the overall experience should be fun. Once I'd settled myself and figured out my topic, I can honestly say that the TEDx Talk was fun. Challenging, but fun.

If you find you're not having fun anymore, maybe it's time to step back, reflect on your thinking, and ask yourself what's happened. Why aren't you having fun anymore? What can you do about it?

I'm not suggesting that everything is a light-hearted game, and nothing is serious. Of course, many of the situations and challenges we face at work need to be taken seriously. But there should still be an element of fun. We should enjoy our work and enjoy our lives at home.

Don't overthink

Next time you're confronted with a situation that leaves you full of anxiety – like me with the TEDx Talk – challenge what your mind is doing. Don't focus on how things might go wrong, what damage might be done, or what the ramifications might be to your image. Take a step back and ask yourself whether you're overthinking this. Could it really be as bad as you imagine? Most of the time, it won't be.

The poet Suzy Kassem wrote: 'doubt has killed more dreams than failure ever will'.

That rings true to me. How many times have you said something about what you wish you could do? How often have you doubted your ability to achieve something? How often have you failed to put yourself forward for something new because you didn't want to fail?

I suggest that you work hard to build confidence in yourself. Believe in yourself and be willing to try new things. Most importantly, try to think like a child. I can guarantee that you're capable of doing all sorts of things you never imagined possible.

Get Comfortable with Silence

As leaders, we often feel that it's up to us to say something if there's a gap in conversation. If we're sitting at the head of the boardroom table, we may feel that people are there to listen to us or are looking to us for direction.

But as a leader, you should spend more time listening than talking. Listen to what your people have to say, listen to their ideas, and listen to their insight. Listening carefully will help you to understand the experiences and frustrations facing your team. Listening means that you're more likely to make good decisions. It also means that you're more likely to understand what people are trying to say, even if they feel they're not able to express it directly.

Alongside listening, learn to ask probing questions that will elicit thoughtful responses from people. You want your team to discuss situations and problems, and you want them to contribute to making thoughtful decisions. This happens through conversation, not through questions that encourage a yes/no response. Once you hone the skill of listening, you'll be able to better lead your team.

I had the pleasure of working alongside a strong listener for several years. We were both board members. Most of the time, this listener just sat quietly and absorbed what was happening. Some people thought he appeared to be disconnected. But whenever he chose to contribute to the conversation, his comments were profound and insightful. He listened closely and he understood the dynamics in the room. He thought carefully before contributing to the conversation. And that meant his input was always highly valuable and impactful.

When you listen closely, you need to listen for understanding, not wait until it's time to respond. So often, people simply listen so they can respond – either to demonstrate that they're part of the conversation or to make sure their own perspective is heard. But true listening is more restrained. Thoughtful listening means that your only goal is to understand what's being said. It's an art form that takes time to develop. It's an approach that requires you to feel comfortable with silence. Developing your skills in close listening will help to set you on the path towards being a great leader.

There are other advantages to remaining silent – beyond just listening to truly understand. If you remain silent and allow others to talk, you'll often find that other people will develop solutions to the challenges they face. By giving your team the freedom to talk without interruption, you can empower them to make their own decisions and feel as though they have a voice in the organisation.

Of course, I'm not suggesting that leaders should always be silent! But remember that listening is powerful, and moments of silence can provide opportunities for other people to contribute. If you've got nothing to say, don't feel that you need to speak. If you need time to think about an issue, don't feel that you need to respond immediately. If you don't know the answer to something, don't feel that you can't admit it. You don't always need to have an answer and you don't always need to contribute, but you should always be ready to listen.

What Is Strategic Thinking?

Defining strategic thinking isn't easy. An online search quickly shows that there's no single, widely accepted definition of what strategic thinking actually involves.

A 2016 article by Nina Bowman in *Harvard Business Review* is a good illustration of this.[26] Bowman opens the article with an example of someone in their performance review being told they needed to be a more strategic thinker. When the person asked what this meant, their manager suggested they needed to think more about the bigger picture behind their work. The trouble with this approach is that it doesn't explain what it takes to be a strategic thinker or how someone can develop strategic thinking skills.

To me, a useful and simple definition of strategic thinking is to see it as an ability to look towards the future and use that future perspective to influence what you do now. It's about developing an approach relevant to today's work, which will guide you towards long-term success and sustainability.

---

26. '4 Ways to Improve Your Strategic Thinking Skills' by Nina A Bowman, 27 December 2016, *Harvard Business Review* (https://hbr.org/2016/12/4-ways-to-improve-your-strategic-thinking-skills).

Strategic thinking is most likely to be useful if it focuses about three to five years ahead. Shorter timeframes don't leave you enough time to implement changes and make an impact. But longer timeframes are unlikely to be helpful because of the pace of technological change.

For an organisation, strategic thinking involves looking ahead and asking a series of questions. What will the industry look like? What will the market look like? What political changes are likely? What geographical regions will you operate in? What logistical changes are likely? What technology changes are likely? What do previous trends and changes tell you about what's likely to happen in the future?

Thinking into the future will help you to plan the best way forward. How will you take advantage of the new systems, processes, and technologies as they happen? How will you respond as new opportunities and challenges present themselves?

Strategic thinking requires a sound understanding of what you're doing now. You need sound understanding of your current processes and procedures so you can work from your current position to where you'd like to be in the future. But it also requires creativity – because planning for the future involves thinking about possibilities. It's a step into the unknown.

Another component of strategic thinking is the decision-making it involves. There are many different decision-making models that may be helpful here. The thing that matters most is that strategic decision-making shouldn't be too process oriented or too much like a checklist. Strategic thinking isn't the same as operational thinking, and checklists belong in the operational arena.

Strategic thinking and strategic decision-making are skills that develop from experience. Early in your career, you're most likely to be operationally focused. As you gain experience, your viewpoint is likely to expand and you'll have more ability to think strategically. Instead of focusing only on the day-to-day running of the business, you'll be thinking about how longer-term, broader decisions will affect the business's future.

It's possible that, in the workplace of the future, most of the day-to-day operations will not be done by people. We'll have machines for those tasks, with most of the human capital in the organisation focused on strategic-level tasks. The people in a business will focus on cause and effect, longer-term development, and how to create value. They'll focus on anticipating trends and developing new ways of working. They'll bring creativity into their work.

Strategic thinking goes beyond setting a growth target. It addresses the how and why that sit behind decisions. If your target is to double the size of your business in five years, for example, strategic thinking is the process that helps you to understand how you can grow, how you can remain efficient, and where you can build new markets. It's the process of breaking down every aspect of your business and understanding how it needs to respond to create the future you seek.

Organisational Culture Is Your Responsibility

Organisational culture is one of those things that's frequently discussed yet difficult to define. It's often easier to judge an organisational culture than it is to define it or describe it.

In simple terms, organisational culture is the collective behaviour of the people in the organisation. It's the sum total of how people work together and get along with each other.

In many organisations, leaders try to unify organisational culture through things like mission, vision, and values. Sometimes they focus on trying to ensure that everyone on the leadership team is aligned. Typically, though, most organisations have a culture that varies – different cultures develop within different teams, across different geographical locations, and at different times.

Recognising a strong organisational culture

Organisational culture is difficult to pin down and difficult to define in a concrete way. But it's definitely something people can feel. A strong, positive culture is likely to feel welcoming, purposeful, positive, and focused.

In most cases, a strong organisational culture is linked to a sense of belonging. If you feel that you fit into an organisation, you're likely to be working in a place where the organisational culture is aligned with the way you think. However, feeling that you don't fit doesn't necessarily mean that the overall culture is poor. It may simply mean the culture isn't a good fit for you.

One of the books I've found useful on this topic is Patrick Lencioni's *The Five Dysfunctions of a Team*.[27] Lencioni takes an almost medical approach to understanding teams. He seeks to diagnose team dysfunctions, understand the signs and symptoms of dysfunction, and then provide a viable treatment. His approach is useful in identifying what's needed to create a strong organisational culture. In this section, I summarise Lencioni's five signs and symptoms of team dysfunction in relation to organisational culture.

1. Absence of trust indicates a dysfunctional culture

If trust is absent within a team or across an organisation, people will be wary about what they say and do. They'll withhold information and resist sharing valuable information because they don't trust their co-workers. They'll always be on guard, never able to relax into their roles.

If you're trying to build a strong organisational culture, you need to develop trust as a foundational element. You need to demonstrate that you trust your team, and you need to demonstrate that you are trustworthy. Over time, this will develop into a strong culture of trust.

2. Fear of conflict indicates a dysfunctional culture

If team members fear conflict, they won't be willing to speak out if they believe something could be improved. They may fear they'll be targeted or excluded because they're rocking

---

27. *The Five Dysfunctions of a Team: A Leadership Fable* by Patrick Lencioni, 2002, John Wiley & Sons.

the boat. They may fear the longer-term consequences of being labelled as a troublemaker. They'll resist questioning things or suggesting new ideas, even when their suggestions could create an improvement.

In a well-functioning organisational culture, team members feel empowered enough to speak out about issues and suggest new ways of working. Usually, these team members have the organisation's best interests at heart, and they speak out because they want to see the organisation improve.

To nurture an environment where staff have little fear of conflict, you need to demonstrate that speaking out does not create risks to the individual, with conflict its inevitable consequence. If you welcome questions and challenges, this culture will gradually permeate throughout the organisation.

3. Lack of commitment indicates a dysfunctional culture

In some organisations, staff appear to be busy doing a lot of things, but they rarely appear to achieve concrete outcomes. There's a general sense that most staff don't know what other staff are working on. There may be a high level of ambiguity in the workplace, perhaps combined with a reluctance to take on new projects.

In a well-functioning organisational culture, each person is committed to delivering the requirements of their role because they understand where their own work fits into the wider picture and they understand how everyone contributes to the organisation's overall direction.

4. Avoidance of accountability indicates a dysfunctional culture

Sometimes staff refuse to be held accountable for something that clearly fits within their role description. This can be reinforced by an unskilled leader who doesn't feel comfortable about holding people to account for their achievements.

Without a clear commitment and sense of accountability, it's impossible to achieve against key performance indicators and it's unlikely the organisation will achieve its objectives. People need to be held accountable. They also need to understand the incentives and consequences that come with their commitment and achievements.

As a leader, you need to be ready to hold staff to account and have difficult conversations if necessary. It's your job to ensure that everyone in the organisation stays focused on achieving their goals.

5. Poor attention to results indicates a dysfunctional culture

Some organisations pay little attention to results and outcomes. If there are no collective goals and little sense that everyone is working towards the same outcomes, then results and outcomes suddenly seem less important.

But results matter. They're often the difference between an organisation that's on the path to long-term success and an organisation on a path to failure. Focusing on results helps to give staff something to work towards.

Culture is your responsibility

In some ways, everyone who works in an organisation is responsible for contributing to its culture. After all, everyone influences it. Ultimately, though, if you're the leader, then organisational culture is 100 per cent your responsibility. Culture is set at the top, and it's something you need to pay attention to.

I heard a CEO say once that they considered themselves to be a CCO – a Chief Cultural Officer – with this role being more important than the Chief Executive Officer role. It's a useful perspective. It's your job to notice, encourage, and reinforce all the positive aspects of your organisation's culture. And if your culture has problems, then it's your job to fix it. Start by paying attention to your own behaviour and the culture you demonstrate every day.

The majority of your success as a leader hinges on how well you build your team and whether you're successful in maintaining a positive culture. It's something that's worth the effort.

Some decades ago, when I was a new supervisor, I reported to someone who was incredibly toxic and who led through intimidation and threats. No one wanted to work with this person, and that created high staff turnover. Eventually I asked this person's supervisor why they allowed it to continue – particularly as the supervisor was well aware of the problem. The reply from the supervisor was that the toxic leader got results. My concern was whether the cost of those results was worth it. It seemed clear to me that, without a change from this person, the organisation would simply stagnate – never managing to grow or achieve new things. If you can't retain staff, it's near impossible to develop as an organisation.

I was fortunate enough to be transferred to a new part of the organisation, and I didn't find out how that particular situation played itself out. But I was reminded of it recently when I read an article about self-made millionaire Gary Vaynerchuk, who speaks about having the confidence to fire the top people in an organisation if it's needed.[28] Vaynerchuk says that if people are toxic, they need to be removed, no matter how senior they are. He suggests that leaders who don't

---

28. 'Self-Made Millionaire Gary Vaynerchuk: The No. 1 Sign You Might Get Fired – Even if You're the Most Talented Employee' by Tom Popomaronis, 26 March 2019, *CNBC MakeIt* (https://www.cnbc.com/2019/03/26/millionaire-gary-vaynerchuk-why-you-need-to-fire-your-most-talented-employee.html).

remove toxic people are actually condoning their behaviour and sending a message throughout the organisation that the toxic behaviour is acceptable. The leader who accepts toxic behaviour is just as bad as the person who behaves that way.

As a leader, it's important that you feel comfortable about the organisational culture you're modelling and encouraging. And if you're an aspiring leader who is working in an organisation that treats you poorly, maybe you should consider finding a new job. Don't work in an organisation that compromises your integrity.

I once had a conversation with a former colleague who told me that their new job wasn't working out well. They had joined an organisation with poor leadership and unethical behaviour. Someone who had recently left this organisation commented that they didn't realise how bad things were until after they'd left and were able to compare it with their new organisation.

There's a lesson here. Sometimes when we're in a situation, we don't recognise it for what it is. Sometimes it's difficult to know what 'bad' looks like. But, if you're thinking of changing jobs, you want to be sure that you're judging your current position in the most objective way possible. You don't want to change jobs because you're unhappy, only to discover yourself working somewhere worse.

It's important to remember that no matter where you work, you're going to have some conflict in the workplace. It's not possible to escape it. Every workplace has some form of conflict, and what matters most is how it's handled. A good leader can recognise healthy and unhealthy conflict and will know how to harness one and cure the other.

Conclusion

I hope this book has given you food for thought and will help you to develop as a leader. Depending on where you're up to in your leadership journey, you may find that some of the principles I've discussed are more relevant for you than others.

Leadership is a journey, and you'll continue to learn as you move along the path. As you develop as a leader, you may like to return to some of the principles I've discussed and consider whether their relevance has changed for you. You may find that different ideas resonate at different stages of your career.

What I've presented here is a set of principles that currently seem important to me. They reflect my current thinking on the topic. I hope you're able to use my principles to develop your own set of principles that will guide you on your own unique leadership journey. Only you can decide which leadership principles are important for you.

The principles I've covered here are necessarily broad. When you're a leader, everything that happens in the organisation is relevant to your job. It's all your responsibility.

When I was a young private in the US Army, a major once asked me what I was doing. I can't remember exactly what I was doing at the time, but I can remember my response. I said that what I was doing wasn't my job. And his response to me was terrific. He said, 'You're a soldier. Everything is your job.'

That's stuck with me throughout my entire career, and I'm glad it's a lesson I learned when I was very young. As you go through the ranks of any organisation, it's helpful to take the view that everything is your job and everything is your responsibility. Whatever comes across your desk, whatever problem you encounter, and whatever challenge you come upon, it's your job to solve it – or at least make sure that it gets referred to the right person. If you take this approach that everything is your job, you'll increase your likelihood of success. That's the broad concept that underpins everything I've discussed in this book. To me, it's the most important concept of all.

The other thing to remember is that leadership is a journey. You need to be constantly learning and constantly developing your skills. There's no destination – just the journey. The best thing you can do is put yourself in situations where you'll develop your skills and learn new things. Never be afraid to learn, and never be afraid to help others to learn.

I hope that, one day, I'm able to learn something from you.

Suggested Reading

Soldier to Executive: Applying Army Leadership Principles to the Corporate World
by Blake Repine (2020, Blake Repine)

The Five Dysfunctions of a Team: A Leadership Fable
by Patrick Lencioni (2002, John Wiley & Sons)

The Ideal Team Player: How to Recognize and Cultivate the Three Essential Virtues
by Patrick Lencioni (2016, John Wiley & Sons)

The 21 Irrefutable Laws of Leadership: Follow Them and People Will Follow You
by John C Maxwell (2022, Harper Collins)

The 360 Degree Leader
by John C Maxwell (2016, Harper Collins)

Mindset: The New Psychology of Success. How We Can Learn to Fulfill Our Potential
by Carol S Dweck (2006, Random House)

Outliers: The Story of Success
by Malcom Gladwell (2008, Little Brown)

The Tipping Point: How Little Things Can Make a Big Difference
by Malcom Gladwell (2000, Little Brown)

Tribes: We Need You to Lead Us
by Seth Godin (2009, Little Brown)

The Dip: A Little Book That Teaches You When to Quit
by Seth Godin (2007, Portfolio)

Grit: The Power of Passion and Perseverance
by Angela Duckworth (2017, Vermilion)

About the Author

Blake Repine spent more than 18 and a half years in various roles in the US Army before transitioning into the corporate world. He is a Senior Executive and Non-Executive Director with more than 20 years' experience in providing strategic vision, leadership and executive management. Blake has expertise in leadership and building strong, positive organisational cultures. He formulates strategies to drive improvement and innovation across a range of large and diverse organisations. Blake has facilitated growth within organisations by establishing targeted solutions and strategic plans to improve operational efficiency and leadership effectiveness.

As well as having attended multiple leadership courses in the Army, Blake also possesses a Bachelor of Science in Multidisciplinary Studies and a Master of Arts in Management and Leadership from Liberty University, an MBA from Norwich University and a Certificate of Completion in Disruptive Strategy from Harvard Business School. Blake is a Certified Professional with the Australian Human Resources Institute (AHRI), a Member of the Institute of Public Accountants (IPA) and a member of the Australian Institute of Company Director's (AICD).

Blake lives in Australia with his wife and son. In his spare time, Blake enjoys fishing, camping, scuba diving, rock climbing and riding motorcycles with his family. He is also an active volunteer in his community.

www.ingramcontent.com/pod-product-compliance
Lightning Source LLC
Chambersburg PA
CBHW020321010526
44107CB00054B/1933